THE AI TSUNAMI

Farsight
Academy & Press

THE AI TSUNAMI

Are You Next? Get Ready

Riz Thakur

with Claude

INDIA EDITION 2026

Farsight Academy Press

The AI Tsunami

India Edition 2026

Published by Farsight Academy Press, Mumbai

ISBN: 978-93-5759-783-8

Farsight Academy Press

CONTENTS

For Sana.

Claude and I wrote this together.

Both of us make mistakes — I sometimes get things wrong, and Claude sometimes invents facts it presents as truth.

Please verify what matters to you before acting on it.

This is not business advice.

What it is: a warning, written with love, for people who deserve to know what is coming.

PROLOGUE

The Man Who Could See the Wave

Let me tell you about two phones.

The first sat in our home in Mumbai when I was a child. Having a telephone at home was itself a small miracle — neighbours walked over just to use it. To call family in Kolhapur, you didn't simply dial a number. You booked a trunk call. You told the operator you wanted a PP call — a Particular Person call. Then you waited. Sometimes hours. The operator would ring back, the person you needed had been summoned, and you had a few minutes to say everything because every second cost money that felt like a meal.

In our Kolhapur home, the phone had no dial at all. You picked up the handset and an operator came on the line. You told her the number — three digits, that was all — and she connected you to the world.

That was the world I was born into.

Now for the second phone.

Recently, sitting at my desk deep in thought, working with artificial intelligence tools that would have seemed like science fiction twenty years ago, there was a young man a few feet away. He works in my home.

He had an iPhone in his hands — the same model that costs more than a month's salary for most Indians.

He was watching Reels. Someone else's wedding, all colour and noise. His face slack with the easy pleasure of it, lit from below by the screen.

His iPhone has more computing power in its palm than several of my laptops combined. The most powerful tool in human history was in his hands. He had no idea. And sitting there watching him, something like grief arrived — because what is coming is something he has not been warned about, and his unawareness right now is not a luxury. It is a danger.

This book is the attempt to fix that.

• • •

Not a professor. Not a politician. No interest in impressing anyone with technical language or academic credentials.

What I am is this: someone who has lived through every technology surge that has swept through India and the world in the last four decades — not as a spectator, but as a builder, a seller, a person with skin in the game who has felt each tide arrive, sometimes in time to ride it, sometimes a moment too late.

The internet came to India at 7 kilobits per second — a speed so slow that downloading a photograph took longer than cooking dinner. When it jumped to 14.4 kilobits, we celebrated. Those were the days of selling internet connections in Mumbai, leaving the laptop on all night just to download music, building India's first B2B online marketplace before anyone had taught me the word B2B. A venture capitalist walked into our office one day and asked if we needed funding. The word venture capital meant nothing to me yet.

Mobile phones came to Mumbai and the streets thought we were listening to FM radio. Nobody believed you could speak wirelessly to someone across the city. Calls cost sixteen rupees a minute outgoing — in a city where sixteen rupees bought a full meal — and still people lined up at STD booths while we were walking and talking.

An Apple iPod in the hands for a few days, early on, and the thought came: a phone is coming from Apple that will combine this with mobile.

It did. Across most of the waves, that kind of reading of the current has held.

This is not autobiography. It is the basis for what follows, because what follows requires you to trust that the person saying it is not prone to exaggeration. Someone who has ridden the dotcom bust. Watched businesses built get wiped out by new technology. Exited at the wrong time and stayed at the wrong time. Launched things the world was not ready for. Not someone given to alarm. And this is the most alarmed that watchfulness has ever made me.

• • •

Not for myself. There has been the extraordinary luck of witnessing enough waves to have some sense of how to move — how to find the new opportunity inside the disruption, how to adapt. Still figuring it out. Still building. Not done.

The boy watching someone else's wedding on his iPhone is who keeps me awake.

The farmers are who I think of — our family has owned agricultural land for generations, and every holiday of my life has been spent on some farm or another. Men and women toiling from before sunrise, doing the same backbreaking work their parents did, saving nothing, one bad season away from ruin. Every one of them has a mobile phone now. Not one has been told what it can do. Not one has been told what is coming.

Picture the young man in Pune, head down over notes spread across a small desk, studying for a data entry job that will not exist when he graduates. He believes the effort will pay off. Nobody has told him otherwise.

The woman in Chennai who has been running accounts in a small company for eleven years — careful double-entry ledgers, quick command of GST filings, never once late with a payroll, genuinely certain that a skill with numbers is a form of permanence — she has not been told that the software can now do what she does in the time it takes her to open her spreadsheet.

The garment worker in Tirupur. The stitch. The same stitch. Ten thousand times today. Her entire economic value inside that motion. She has not heard of the machine that is already doing it faster, cheaper, and without a lunch break.

The terror is not about the scale of what is coming, though the scale is staggering. It is about the silence. The organised, institutional absence of anyone whose job it is to warn these people, prepare them, catch them before the cliff — while the decisions that will reshape their lives are being made in rooms they will never enter.

• • •

Think about pagers. Small devices that beeped and displayed a number, telling you to find a telephone and call someone back. An entire industry. Motorola built a business around them. Pagers were launched in India. And then mobile phones came — not better pagers, but something from a completely different category — and the pager industry did not decline slowly and gracefully. It was erased. Motorola went from dominant to cautionary tale in what felt like a single exhale.

The people who made pagers did not see it coming from within the pager industry. It came from outside. It always comes from outside.

Artificial intelligence is not a better version of something that already exists. It is something from a completely different category. And it is not coming for one industry. It is coming for dozens simultaneously. Unlike every previous surge — the internet, mobile, apps, cloud — this one is moving faster than human institutions, governments, education systems, and families can adapt.

The first time I used ChatGPT — one of the early AI tools that is now common — I sat back and felt something shift. For the first time in a technology career, here was a system that could keep up with my thoughts. Not because my thoughts are important. Because I have spent decades building systems, thinking three steps ahead of what available infrastructure could support. And suddenly here was a system that did not ask me to slow down. That met me where I was. That then went further.

If it can do that for someone who has spent decades in technology — imagine what it does to the job that requires no technology background. The task done the same way every day by a person whose only asset is the willingness to keep showing up and doing it.

• • •

Here is the simplest way to explain what is at stake.

The poor are poor because they sell minutes. A garment worker repeats a single stitch every few seconds. A data entry clerk types the same information into the same field hundreds of times a day. A security guard walks the same perimeter at the same time every night. Their entire economic value lives inside a short, repeating loop.

People who have built large things — entrepreneurs, executives, innovators — they also repeat. But their cycles are long. A strategic decision repeated quarterly. A fundraise every few years. A product repositioning every decade. The loop is long enough, complex enough, contextual enough, that a machine cannot yet close it cleanly.

THE SHORTER YOUR REPETITION CYCLE, THE CLOSER YOU ARE TO THE CLIFF.

This book will not comfort. Its purpose is to wake. There is no interest in saying everything will be fine, because that is not something anyone can know. What is known is that people who understand what is coming have a fighting chance. The people still sleeping — distracted, comfortable, assuming that because things have always found a way to work out they always will — they are the ones this is most urgently for.

• • •

Mine is a generation that is rare. I held a telephone with no dial. Watched the internet arrive at the speed of cold honey. Launched mobile phones in a city that didn't believe wireless calling was real. Built things before the words for them existed. Watched this country transform in ways our grandparents could not have imagined in their most extravagant dreams.

What is coming next is different. Not different in the way that each new technology is different. Different in scale. Different in speed.

Different in who it will affect and how completely it will affect them.

THE WATER IS COMING.

Put the phone down. And read what follows.

— The Author

CHAPTER 1: THE MAN AT THE GATE

CHAPTER 1

THE MAN AT THE GATE

LIFTMEN. SECURITY GUARDS. WATCHMEN. AGNIVEERS. TEN MILLION PEOPLE. ZERO WARNING OF WHAT IS COMING.

Let me ask you something you have never been asked before.

When did you last see a liftman?

Not a security guard at the entrance. Not the concierge at the front desk. A liftman — the specific person employed to stand inside a lift, press the button for your floor, and smile politely as the doors closed. A person whose entire job was to do one thing that the lift could already do by itself.

If you live in one of the newer residential towers built in the last five years — in Mumbai, Pune, Bengaluru, Gurgaon — your answer is probably: I have not seen one in years. The lift opens by itself, reads your access card, takes you to your floor. You did not notice the liftman disappear. He was simply gone one day, replaced so quietly that his absence felt like an upgrade rather than a loss.

But drive a few kilometres from those towers. Enter the buildings of the previous decade — the ones with marble lobbies but older systems, staffed by men in pressed uniforms rather than cameras with sensors. There, in the lift, you will still find him. Sitting on a small stool. Ready to press 12 for you before your hand reaches the panel.

And when you step out of that lift and walk toward the building exit, who is sitting at the gate? The watchman. Sometimes it is even the same man — the liftman who lost his post in the building that upgraded, and found a new posting as a watchman in the building next door that had not. The job changed. The person did not. He adapted the only way he knew how: he moved one step sideways, to the next available role.

That watchman at the gate is who this chapter is about. And the question this chapter asks is: when the gate automates too — and it is already automating — where does he go next?

There is nowhere left to go sideways.

• • •

THE THESIS IN HUMAN FORM

In the framework of this book — the idea that the shorter your repetition cycle, the closer you are to being replaced — the liftman was the most extreme case imaginable. His cycle was measured in seconds. Button pressed. Doors opened. Button pressed again. A loop so short and so mechanical that to an engineer designing an automation system, it was not a job description. It was a test case.

The watchman's cycle is only slightly longer. Someone arrives at the gate. He checks if they have a reason to be there. He lets them in or he does not. He does this dozens of times a shift. Walk the perimeter. Check the gate. Walk the perimeter again. This is his day. This is his night. This has been his life for five years, or eight years, or twelve.

For decades, this was fine — because the cost of automating that gate was higher than the cost of paying the man to stand at it. That calculation has now changed. In some buildings it changed three years ago. In others it is changing this year. Building by building, society by society, as each management committee looks at the numbers and finds that a camera system pays for itself within a year and then works for a decade without a salary, a holiday, or a provident fund contribution.

• • •

HOW MANY PEOPLE ARE WE TALKING ABOUT

India's private security industry employs somewhere between nine and twelve million people. This makes it the second-largest employer in the country, after agriculture. Pause on that number. More people earn their living guarding doors, gates, and buildings than work in all of India's much-celebrated technology sector. This workforce is larger than the Army, Navy, Air Force, and Police combined. There are five private security personnel for every one police officer in the country.

Most of them come from four states: Odisha, Bihar, Uttar Pradesh, Jharkhand. They earn between fifteen thousand and twenty-five thousand rupees a month. They send money home. They share a room in the city with two or three others. They work twelve-hour shifts without complaint, because the alternative is no shift at all.

The industry has a thirty-two percent annual attrition rate — meaning roughly one in three guards leaves or is replaced every year. This is not because the work is impossible. It is because the work is grinding, the pay is low, and there is no visible path forward. The man who joins as a watchman at twenty-five is, in most cases, still a watchman at thirty-five. The job does not grow.

What none of these men have been told is that the job itself is about to shrink.

• • •

THE NUMBERS BEHIND THE DECISION

Let me show you exactly how the decision to replace a watchman gets made, because it is not a dramatic moment. It happens in a building society AGM, in a line item on a spreadsheet, when a facilities manager presents a comparison to the committee.

The true cost of employing one security guard — including salary, Provident Fund contribution, ESI, uniform, training, and the overhead of managing the position — is approximately three and a half to four lakh rupees per year. A typical residential society runs three guards across day and night shifts. That is ten to twelve lakh rupees a year, every year, for three people watching a gate.

An AI camera system with facial recognition and an automated boom barrier costs around six to eight lakh rupees, installed. It then connects to a remote monitoring centre for about one and a half lakh per year. Year One total: roughly eight lakh. Year Two onwards: one and a half lakh per year.

The system replaces three guards costing twelve lakh a year with a setup that costs eight lakh once and one and a half lakh every year after. The capital pays back in under twelve months.

After that, the society saves nine to ten lakh rupees every single year, permanently.

There is no spreadsheet on which this decision is unclear. The only reason it has not already swept through every building in every city is awareness — the committee that has not yet seen the calculation, the facilities manager who has not yet been shown the product. Awareness is spreading. Decisions are being made. The math does not wait.

• • •

WHAT THE CAMERA ACTUALLY DOES

I want to be precise about what exists today — not what technology might do in five years, but what is already working in buildings right now.

A facial recognition camera at a gate does not just take a photograph. It checks the face it sees against a database of residents and registered guests, makes a decision in under a second, and either opens the boom barrier or keeps it closed. It does this a thousand times a day without getting distracted, without getting tired, and without being charmed by someone who claims to know Mrs. Sharma on the twelfth floor.

AI-enabled cameras watch a building the way no human being can. A conventional CCTV camera records footage for someone to review after an incident. An AI camera watches in real time and flags anomalies — a person standing in the same spot for too long, a vehicle parked where vehicles are not permitted, movement near the back gate at 2am. It watches every corner simultaneously, always, without the 4am drowsiness that any honest security company will admit is an industry-wide reality.

And here is the economic insight that makes this irresistible: one trained operator sitting at a remote monitoring centre can manage the camera feeds of twelve to fifteen buildings at once. Twelve buildings that each employed two night guards now require one operator and a monthly software fee. The mathematics are not complicated. They are simply uncomfortable.

• • •

THE MACHINE YOU CANNOT CHARM

There is something about full automation that goes beyond the economics, and it is the observation that security professionals know but rarely say publicly.

A significant number of security failures are not the result of force. They are the result of conversation. Someone talks their way past a guard. A fake ID receives only a cursory look. Someone says 'I am from the third floor, just let me up.' Someone tips the guard fifty rupees. Someone arrives in a uniform that looks approximately correct.

The human guard is a social being. He is subject to politeness, to embarrassment about confrontation, to the natural human reluctance to stop someone who seems confident and in a hurry. These are not character flaws. They are the conditions of being human. And they are precisely the conditions that determined visitors — authorised or not — learn to use.

When every person approaching a gate knows that a camera will check their face before it opens, that a record exists of every entry, and that there is no human being to negotiate with, something changes. Not just for people who should not be there. For everyone. Behaviour adjusts before the gate, not at it.

This is what security professionals call the psychology of machine authority. The camera cannot be charmed. It cannot be reasoned with. It cannot be made to feel that stopping you would be awkward. It simply checks, and decides, and the gate either opens or it does not. And most people, knowing this, follow the process rather than test it.

The situations that require genuine human judgment — a medical emergency in the lobby, a distressed resident at the gate at midnight, a dispute that needs de-escalation — those still need a person. But in the new model, that person is a trained rapid-response officer, better paid and better equipped than the watchman he replaces, deployed only when a human being is actually needed. The automation funds the upgrade.

• • •

YOUR COUSIN'S VISIT – A PICTURE OF WHERE WE ARE GOING

Let me make this concrete. Let me show you exactly what the near-future of a residential building looks like – not a concept, but a system using technology that already exists commercially today.

You live in a thirty-floor building in Mumbai. Your cousin is visiting from Pune for the first time. You send him a digital guest pass from your building's app: his name, which flat he is visiting, his arrival window, which floors he may access. That is the full extent of your involvement.

Your cousin arrives at the gate. What happens next involves no human guard at any point.

A facial recognition camera checks his face against the guest database. Your digital invitation is found. The boom barrier opens. A small drone – sitting charged in a pod near the gate, the size of a lunchbox – lifts quietly into the air and follows him as he walks into the compound. He does not know it is there. It maintains a respectful distance, four metres behind him, its cameras tracking.

A calm voice from the drone says: 'Please proceed to Lift Bank B on your right. You are authorised for Floor 24.' The lobby cameras confirm his face matches the invited guest. Sensors in the ceiling track him from one zone to the next.

Your cousin, curious, wanders toward the swimming pool. The drone says: 'This area is for residents only. Please return to Lift Bank B.' On your phone, a notification arrives: 'Your guest has moved toward the pool area at 2:32pm.' If he ignores the prompt, an alert reaches the remote monitoring centre and the drone keeps tracking.

The lift accepts only Floor 24 as a valid destination for his visitor pass. He arrives. The corridor camera confirms he is moving toward your flat. Heat sensors on the ceiling track a single authorised visitor moving in the expected direction. The entire floor is monitored without a human being standing in a corridor.

When his two-hour window ends, a notification goes to both of you. He leaves. The gate opens as his face approaches. His pass is logged as completed and deactivated. The whole visit – entry to exit — is tracked, recorded, and managed, and no watchman was involved at any point.

Every component I have described — the facial recognition gate, the autonomous drone, the heat sensors, the visitor pass app — is commercially available today. The drone pod alone costs twenty to thirty lakh rupees. The full system for a large residential complex costs less than the three-year salary bill of the guards it replaces. And unlike those guards, it does not have a thirty-two percent attrition rate.

• • •

THE FENCE THAT FEELS YOU COMING

Beyond the gate and the lobby, there is a world of perimeter security that most people have never had reason to think about. The technology for it was, until recently, the exclusive property of military installations and border posts. Then the price fell. And fell again.

A fibre optic cable running along the length of a fence can detect intrusion — cutting, climbing, pressing — to within three metres, and classify what it is detecting. A person cutting a fence produces a different vibration signature from a dog leaning against it, or wind moving through it. The system does not just detect. It identifies. And it is always alert, at every metre of the fence, simultaneously.

When the sensor triggers, an autonomous drone launches from its charging pod and reaches the flagged location in under a minute. Its cameras — one standard, one thermal — show the remote operator exactly what is happening, in the dark if necessary. The drone's speaker challenges the intruder. The rapid response team receives GPS coordinates. The drone tracks until they arrive.

Three men attempted to cut through the rear fence of a manufacturing estate in Pune at 3am last year. The fibre optic sensor flagged the cutting vibration at the first cut. The drone was overhead in forty-five seconds. The operator called the police with live GPS coordinates. Two men were apprehended.

Three guards doing regular patrols on a large estate would almost certainly not have been at that section of fence at that moment. The sensor is always at every section of fence. That is a difference that cannot be bridged by adding more guards.

• • •

WHAT COULD BE BUILT

I do not want to leave this chapter only as a warning. The people who read this book carefully are also the people who could build what needs to be built. Three clear opportunities exist.

The first is in the transition itself. The industry is moving from twenty guards to four — but those four are doing something fundamentally different. The remote monitoring operator who manages twelve buildings from a control room is not a guard. He is a trained analyst who reads AI alerts, coordinates rapid response, and makes the human calls that the system flags for judgment. This role requires basic technology literacy and calm under pressure. Many current security guards have the calm and the discipline. They do not yet have the training. A short, practical, phone-based reskilling programme — in Hindi, Odia, Bhojpuri — that prepares a security guard to become a monitoring operator rather than become unemployed is a genuine business, addressing a genuine need, that nobody is adequately serving today.

The second opportunity connects to a large pool of young people entering the workforce every year through military and paramilitary service. Tens of thousands of trained, disciplined, physically capable young men complete short-tenure service stints and look for civilian work each year. A focused placement and reskilling network that directs these men toward roles that automation cannot easily fill — rapid response, emergency management, high-value logistics security, drone operation — builds careers rather than dead ends. The entrepreneur who builds this creates value for the young men, for the security industry, and for the economy.

The third opportunity is the integrator. The new security model — AI monitoring plus human rapid response — needs a business that packages and sells it as a complete product, not as a set of components that each building society must figure out how to combine. A hybrid security company that offers AI-first monitoring with human backup, priced against what buildings currently spend on full human guarding, is a business that practically writes its own pitch deck. The technology is available. The trained human component can be built. The market is enormous and largely unaddressed.

• • •

THE CLOSE

Let me take you back to the man in the lift.

Some of those men, when their building upgraded, became watchmen. They moved one step sideways to the next available role, the way people have always moved when the specific thing they were doing became unnecessary — adapting, staying employed, continuing to provide for their families. This is not failure. This is resourcefulness.

But the watchman at the gate is standing at the last sideways step. The gate is automating. There is no role to the left of watchman that a camera cannot fill more cheaply.

The man from Odisha who has been at his post for four years, who sends eight thousand rupees home every month, who has a plan for his daughter's schooling — he is not aware that his building society committee has a technology proposal on the agenda. He has no particular reason to be. Nobody in his industry, his community, or his government has thought it their responsibility to warn him.

This is the silence the uncle in me cannot accept. Not the automation. Not the economics. The silence. The organised, institutional absence of any warning to the people who need it most, while the decisions that will reshape their lives are made in committee rooms they will never enter.

The water is not coming. For this sector, for the man at the gate, it is already here. The question is only whether anyone is going to warn him in time for him to do something about it.

I began with the building gate because the building gate is something every Indian reader passes through every day. The man standing at it has a face you can already picture. His displacement, when it comes, will at least be visible — it will be noticed, debated, covered in newspapers. He is in the city. People will eventually pay attention.

Now I need to take you somewhere the cameras do not follow. Away from the lobby and the gate and the building society AGM. Away from the city entirely.

I need to take you to a field at five in the morning, where a man has been bent at the waist since before sunrise, doing the same motion his father did and his grandfather did, on land that is being quietly surrounded by forces he has never heard of. Where six hundred million people live and work. Where the displacement will be so large, and so dispersed, that when it happens nobody will be in a position to count who was lost.

Come with me to the farm.

• • •

CHAPTER 2

THE PHONE IN HIS POCKET

AGRICULTURE & FARMING

Let me take you somewhere at five in the morning.

Not to a boardroom. Not to a startup office in Bangalore. To a field in Maharashtra, one hour outside Pune, where I am standing next to my neighbour watching him work.

He has been awake since four. He owns three buffalos and two cows. He has milked them already — his hands moving through motions he has repeated ten thousand times, the same grip, the same rhythm, a knowledge that lives in muscle memory the way your fingers know a phone number without thinking. He will sell the milk to the local dairy for forty rupees a litre. Sometimes forty-five if the buyer is generous. He has done this for twenty years. His father did it before him.

He does not know what cheese is.

I do not mean he has not tasted it. I mean the concept itself that milk can be transformed into a product selling for eight hundred rupees per kilogram in Mumbai, fifteen hundred in some shops in Bandra and Bangalore — this information has never reached him. He has heard of paneer. Of course. But that is made in the city. By companies. Not by a man with five animals and a small plot of land.

Now look at what is in his pocket. A smartphone. Not an old Nokia. A smartphone. The same device that urban children use to order food, book cabs, watch movies, learn languages. The same device that has more computing power than the laptops that sent humans to the moon.

He uses it to make phone calls. Sometimes he watches videos his nephew sends him. He does not know — and this is what keeps me awake at night — he does not know that this phone in his pocket could tell him which crop will fetch the best price eight weeks from now. How to grow kale, which restaurants in Pune are paying four hundred rupees per kilogram for. Where the nearest training exists to learn cheese-making. That his tomatoes, instead of rotting during the harvest glut when prices crash to five rupees a kilo, could be dehydrated and sold for three hundred rupees year-round.

This gap — between the tool in his hand and the knowledge of what it can do — is not unique to my neighbour. It is the defining crisis of six hundred million people in India who depend on agriculture for their survival.

• • •

THE SCALE

Approximately six hundred million Indians depend on agriculture. Not work in agriculture. Depend on it. Their food. Their children's education. Their survival. This is nearly half of India's population.

Of these, one hundred and forty-four million are landless agricultural labourers. They own nothing. Not the field they work in. Not the seed they plant. They sell their hands, their backs, their daylight hours for two hundred and fifty to four hundred rupees a day. When there is work. When there is no work, they earn nothing. No savings. No buffer. One bad season away from crisis.

The average farm in India is less than two hectares — roughly the size of three football fields. Most farmers are not agricultural businesspeople. They are families trying to survive on land too small to generate real wealth, in a system designed to extract value from them rather than build it for them.

Most small farmers operate without a week's cash reserve. Every harvest is survival or catastrophe. There is no middle ground.

• • •

THE MACHINES ARE ALREADY HERE

Let me tell you what is happening in fields across India right now. Not in five years. Not in a decade. Now.

In Punjab, drones spray pesticides across twenty acres in the time it used to take ten labourers an entire day. The drone costs the farmer three thousand rupees to hire for the day. The ten labourers used to cost four thousand total — plus food, plus supervision, plus the risk that they might not show up at all.

A woman in her fifties who has spent thirty years bending over paddy fields, transplanting seedlings, earning three hundred rupees a day — her work is being replaced by a rice transplanting machine that can plant four acres in the time she plants a quarter acre. The machine does not get a backache. It does not take lunch breaks. It does not need to be paid separately for overtime.

In Haryana and parts of Maharashtra, combine harvesters that cost a farmer five thousand rupees a day replace the twenty to thirty harvest workers who used to manually cut, bundle, and load the crop. The workers earned two hundred and fifty to three hundred rupees each. The math is clear. The farmer saves money. The workers lose their daily wage.

These workers — the woman transplanting seedlings, the men cutting wheat — are the most vulnerable people in this book. They own no land. They have no asset to fall back on. Their entire economic value lives in the repetition of a physical task that a machine now performs faster, cheaper, and without rest. When the machine arrives on a farm, they do not get a notice. They simply stop being called.

And the machine is arriving. Not as a distant possibility. As a present reality. India imported over forty-five thousand combine harvesters and rice transplanting machines in the last five years. The government subsidises their purchase. The farmer who can afford them buys them. The labourers who used to do that work look for the next available job — and find, increasingly, that the next available job is also being automated.

• • •

THE TRAP THE FARMER CANNOT SEE

The farmer-owner faces a different kind of threat. Not the immediate replacement of his labour, but the slow, invisible collapse of the economics he depends on.

He does not plant what the market needs. He plants what his neighbour planted last year. If the neighbour did reasonably well with onions, he plants onions. If the neighbour made money on tomatoes, he plants tomatoes. This is not because he is unintelligent or lazy. This is survival arithmetic. You cannot afford to experiment when your family's survival depends on this one harvest. You copy what worked for someone you trust.

The problem is that everyone is doing the same calculation. If onions did well last season, two hundred farmers in the district plant onions this season. Supply floods the market. Prices crash. Everyone earns less than the cost of cultivation.

But the farmer does not have visibility into this until he arrives at the mandi — the wholesale market — with his produce. Only then does he discover that the price is half of what he hoped, a quarter of what he needed.

By then it is too late.

The mandi trader, sitting on the other side of the transaction, has full information. He knows the volumes arriving that day from every district. He knows the prices in the city. He knows what buyers are willing to pay. The farmer knows none of this. He has travelled with his produce, often overnight, often at his own expense, and he must sell today because he has no cold storage and no way to take the produce home. The trader makes his offer. The farmer accepts it or watches his produce rot.

Typically three to five middlemen stand between the farmer and the urban consumer. Each extracts a margin. By the time the tomato that left the farm at five rupees a kilo reaches a Mumbai supermarket at eighty rupees a kilo, the farmer has received less than seven percent of what the consumer paid. The other ninety-three percent was absorbed by traders, transporters, wholesalers, and retailers — none of whom grew anything.

The farmer feeds this country and receives the smallest share of what his food is worth. This has been true for decades. What is changing is not the injustice. What is changing is the scale and speed of the forces that will make it worse.

• • •

THE OPPORTUNITY HE HAS NEVER BEEN TOLD ABOUT

While the machines replace his labour and the mandi system extracts his margin, there is an entirely separate crisis unfolding — one of invisible opportunity.

Every morning, my neighbour produces about fifteen to eighteen litres of milk from his five animals. At forty-five rupees a litre, that is roughly eight hundred rupees a day. About twenty-four thousand rupees a month if he sells every day.

Now let me show you what that same milk could become.

From one hundred litres of milk, you can make about ten kilograms of cheese. My neighbour produces approximately five hundred and forty litres a month. That could theoretically yield fifty-four kilograms of cheese. Artisanal cheese in India sells for anywhere between six hundred and fifteen hundred rupees per kilogram. At a conservative eight hundred rupees per kilogram, fifty-four kilograms generates forty-three thousand rupees. Almost double his current income. From the same milk. The same animals. The same daily work.

But making cheese requires knowledge he does not have. It requires equipment he does not own — a basic cheese making set-up costs between fifty thousand and one and a half lakh rupees. It requires training. It requires customers — and he does not know where to find the premium buyers in Pune and Mumbai who will pay eight hundred rupees for artisanal cheese.

So he sells the milk for forty-five rupees a litre. And in Chennai, an IIM graduate who quit her corporate job runs Käse, an artisanal cheese company that sources milk from ethical farmers, makes forty varieties, and sells them at premium prices online and in gourmet stores. She won a silver award at the World Cheese Awards in Norway.

In Gujarat, young pastoral shepherds at Panchal Dairy are trained to make cheese from goat and sheep milk, selling chevre and tomme to urban customers willing to pay for quality. In Rajasthan, a project called Camel Charisma makes cheese from camel milk provided by Raika herders — supporting a fading pastoral tradition while creating a premium product.

These cheesemakers exist. They are building successful businesses. But none of them are traditional dairy farmers. They are educated, city-connected entrepreneurs who learned about the opportunity, learned the craft, and built the business. The dairy farmer milking his animals at 5am was never part of this conversation.

The same pattern repeats across every crop. Restaurants in Pune, Gurgaon, and Hyderabad buy exotic vegetables — zucchini, bell peppers, broccoli, cherry tomatoes — at five to ten times the price of regular vegetables. This market exceeds two billion dollars in India and is growing. Microgreens — baby versions of vegetables and herbs grown in trays — take seven to fourteen days from seed to harvest, require minimal space, and sell to restaurants for extraordinary prices. The market is growing at twenty percent a year.

The farmer with two acres does not know microgreens exist.

The market exists. The premium-paying customer exists. The farmer capable of learning exists. What does not exist is the bridge between them.

• • •

THE URBAN ENTREPRENEUR IS COMING FOR THE FARM

Here is something that should alarm every small farmer in India, except they do not know it is happening.

In Hyderabad, an entrepreneur who studied at a prestigious engineering college runs thirty vertical farms across the city. These are not fields. These are warehouses with controlled environments — temperature, humidity, light — all managed by sensors and software. He grows fifty different crops year-round. No dependence on monsoon. No pest attacks. Water usage is ninety percent less than traditional farming. Yield per square foot is thirty times higher. He sells fresh produce to restaurants within hours of harvest, with margins of thirty to forty percent.

In Bangalore, another entrepreneur uses hydroponics — growing vegetables in nutrient-rich water, no soil required — in a warehouse a few kilometres from the city centre. Kale, lettuce, microgreens, basil. Multiple harvests per year. Direct sales to gourmet stores and high-end restaurants.

These people are not competing with traditional farmers by being better at farming. They are competing by being better at technology, better at market access, better at branding. They studied which crops fetch premium prices. They learned the techniques from YouTube and online courses. They set up near cities, close to their premium buyers. They hired people with commerce backgrounds, not agriculture backgrounds, to run their operations.

And they are winning.

The traditional farmer with two acres and twenty years of experience does not even know this competition exists. He is still planting what his neighbour planted, hoping for rain, hoping for a decent price at the mandi. While urban entrepreneurs with no family history in agriculture build tech-enabled farms that out-produce, out-price, and out-deliver him.

Technology is not coming to agriculture. Technology is already here. The question is: who gets to use it? Who gets trained? Who gets financed? Who gets access? Right now, the answer is the people who already have education, capital, and connections. The traditional small farmer is being left behind — not because he is incapable, but because no one is investing in making him capable.

• • •

THE CHEVON LESSON

Before I tell you what farmers could do, I need to tell you what I did. Not to impress you. To establish that I am not speaking as someone who has read reports and attended conferences.

I own Chevon — a branded packaged goat meat business that addresses an unorganised market. When we started, every single advisor told us we were wrong to freeze the meat. 'Fresh is what Indian consumers want,' they said. 'Freezing will make the meat tough. You will lose the market to fresh meat vendors.'

We ignored them.

Because freezing is not about the meat. Freezing is about time and space. A fresh product has a shelf life of hours to days. A frozen product has a shelf life of months to a year. Fresh meat can only be sold within a few kilometres of where the animal was slaughtered. Frozen meat can be shipped a thousand kilometres and still arrive in perfect condition.

Fresh means you are trapped by geography and time. Frozen means you can reach any customer, anywhere in the country, and sell when the price is right — not when the inventory is about to spoil.

Now apply that lesson to agriculture. A tomato farmer harvests during the season. Everyone in his region harvests tomatoes at the same time. Supply floods the market. Prices crash to five or eight rupees a kilo. He has no cold storage. He has no processing unit. So he sells at whatever price the trader offers, because the alternative is watching his tomatoes rot.

If that same farmer had access to a small dehydration unit — an electric dryer that costs one to two lakh rupees, subsidised by the government at thirty-five percent — he could dehydrate the tomatoes. Dehydrated tomato powder sells for three hundred to six hundred rupees per kilogram. The same tomatoes he was getting eight rupees for, processed, become worth forty to seventy times more. And they do not spoil. He can sell in the off-season when prices are high. He can sell online. He can sell to restaurants and food companies.

The raw material is not the constraint. The market demand is not the constraint. The constraint is knowledge — knowing that processing exists, that subsidies exist, that markets exist, and that you have the ability to access all of it. That gap is what this chapter is about.

• • •

THE STORAGE THE GOVERNMENT WILL PAY FOR — THAT NO ONE KNOWS ABOUT

Here is something that will make you angry. It should.

India loses ninety-two thousand crore rupees worth of food every year. Fruits and vegetables rotting before they reach the market. Onions piled in the open, thirty to thirty-five percent spoiling for lack of proper storage. Tomatoes that could have fed families or generated income, wasted.

At the same time, the Indian government has built eight thousand six hundred and eighty-nine cold storage facilities across the country, with a total capacity of thirty-seven million metric tonnes. The government has allocated more than one lakh crore rupees for agricultural infrastructure through various schemes. Subsidies cover thirty-five to fifty percent of the capital cost for setting up cold storage. Interest-free loans up to two crore rupees are available for building post-harvest infrastructure.

The schemes exist. The money is real. The infrastructure is being built.

But most small farmers do not know any of it exists.

PMKSY, MIDH, AIF — these are the scheme names. The farmer milking his buffalos at 5am has never heard these acronyms. He has never been told that the government will subsidise the dryer that could multiply his tomato income forty times. Nobody sat with him, in his language, and explained that this money exists, how to apply for it, and what it could do for his family.

The schemes exist. The money is real. The knowledge transfer does not exist. And money that farmers do not know about might as well not exist.

• • •

THE AI SOLUTION: A PLATFORM BUILT FOR THE SMALLHOLDER

Everything I have described so far is the problem. The awareness gap. The knowledge gap. The training gap. The market access gap. Now let me tell you about the solution I am building — not theoretically, but actually.

Component One: Crop Intelligence and Forward Price Prediction.

Imagine this: a farmer in Pune opens WhatsApp. He receives a voice message in Marathi. The message says: 'This season, satellite data shows heavy onion planting across your district. Supply will be high. Wholesale prices are predicted to drop to twelve to fifteen rupees per kilo in eight weeks. But kale demand is growing in Pune restaurants. Current wholesale price is three hundred and eighty rupees per kilo. Here is a three-minute video on how to grow kale. Here is the contact for a buyer who will guarantee purchase. Consider switching.'

This is not science fiction. Every piece of technology needed to deliver this message exists today. The government's Agmarknet database has wholesale mandi prices for every market, every day, going back years. Satellite data from Sentinel-2 — free, from the European Space Agency — estimates crop coverage and volumes across any district in India. Consumer demand data exists through modern retail chains and online food delivery platforms. Weather data from the India Meteorological Department is free and public.

An AI takes all of this data, models historical patterns, accounts for current planting data, and predicts with reasonable accuracy what the wholesale price will be four to eight weeks from now. Not perfectly. But well enough to help a farmer make better decisions than he is making today — which is copying his neighbour and hoping for the best. The prediction is delivered via voice, in the local language, on WhatsApp. No app to download. No dashboard to learn. A voice message the farmer listens to with his morning tea.

Component Two: Guaranteed Purchase Price.

The government runs a Minimum Support Price programme. The idea is sound: guarantee farmers a floor price so they are not exploited by traders. The reality is broken. The MSP covers twenty-three crops, but only twenty to twenty-five percent of farmers know it exists. Of those, only a fraction can actually sell to government procurement agencies because the infrastructure does not exist everywhere, the paperwork is burdensome, and implementation is unreliable.

The private equivalent — a direct relationship between farmers and buyers, with a guaranteed purchase price agreed before planting — solves this without government dependency. The farmer knows, before he puts a single seed in the ground, what price he will receive and who will buy his crop. He can plan. He can invest. He can take a calculated risk rather than blindly copying his neighbour.

Component Three: Accessible Financing.

A farmer who receives forward price intelligence and a guaranteed buyer still needs capital to grow the new crop — to buy the seed, the dryer, the basic processing equipment. Traditional bank loans require paperwork and collateral that most small farmers do not have. A platform that provides small, targeted financing — three to ten lakh rupees — secured against the guaranteed purchase contract rather than land title, reaches the farmers that the banking system has never served.

Component Four: Drones and IoT on the Ground.

The intelligence layer tells the farmer what to grow and what the price will be. The fourth component tells him how his crop is actually doing. Soil sensors, drone monitoring, satellite crop health analysis — all of these produce data that a farmer's grandfather could not have imagined, and all of it is now cheap enough to be genuinely accessible. A drone that monitors crop health across twenty acres and flags early signs of disease or water stress costs the farmer three thousand rupees to hire for the day. The alternative is discovering the problem three weeks later when it is too late.

• • •

CAN THE FARMER ACTUALLY DO THIS?

I know what you are thinking. This is all very well. But the farmer I described at the opening of this chapter — the man milking his buffalos at 5am, who does not know what cheese is — can he actually navigate an AI platform, access a guaranteed buyer, and apply for financing?

Honestly: not alone, and not immediately. That would be asking him to make a decade's worth of transitions in one harvest.

But the apprenticeship model works. One farmer in a village who sees the platform working, who takes the risk of growing kale instead of onions and receives three hundred and eighty rupees a kilogram instead of twenty, who gets a loan and buys a dryer and doubles his tomato income — that farmer becomes the teacher. His neighbours watch. They ask questions. They try. The knowledge spreads the way all agricultural knowledge has always spread: farm to farm, family to family, across fences and over morning tea.

The goal is not to transform six hundred million farmers simultaneously. The goal is to give the first farmer in each village a genuine reason to try something different, and the support to succeed when he does.

Imagine three harvests. In the first harvest, the farmer uses the platform's price intelligence for the first time. He does not change his crop yet — he is watching, testing, checking if the prediction was right. It is. He tells his neighbour. In the second harvest, he tries a small plot of the recommended crop alongside his usual one. He sells it to the guaranteed buyer at the agreed price. He earns more per kilo than he has ever earned. In the third harvest, he makes the full switch. He applies for the dryer subsidy. He processes his surplus. His son, watching all of this, helps him navigate the app.

Three harvests. Two years. One family's trajectory changes. And it does not stop there. The son gets a better education. His daughter finishes college. The next generation enters the economy with assets and skills rather than vulnerability.

This is what I mean by teaching to fish. Not giving the farmer a better price this season. Giving him the tools to secure better prices for the rest of his life.

• • •

WHAT COULD BE BUILT

The platform I have described is one answer. But it is not the only answer. Anyone reading this book who has capital, skills, or energy to spare should see three clear opportunities in Indian agriculture.

The first is last-mile knowledge transfer. Schemes exist. Subsidies are real. Markets are waiting. What does not exist is a trusted human being who sits with a small farmer in his language and explains all of it in plain terms. An organisation that trains and deploys agricultural extension workers — not government officials, but village-level entrepreneurs paid per farmer they successfully connect to a scheme, a buyer, or a training programme

— fills a gap that the entire agritech sector has largely ignored. The rural business correspondent model, which works for banking, can work for agriculture.

The second is the farmer cooperative for value addition. Ten dairy farmers who each have five animals and produce eighteen litres a day collectively produce nine hundred litres a day. One trained cheesemaker, one shared equipment facility, one collective brand. This model works.

Amul proved it for liquid milk over fifty years ago. It has not been seriously replicated for cheese, for dehydrated produce, or for premium-branded grains. The entrepreneur who builds the cooperative infrastructure — the legal templates, the shared equipment financing, the buyer relationships — and licenses it to farmer groups across Maharashtra or Karnataka is solving a genuine and large problem.

The third is the government scheme navigator. Most farmers never access the subsidies they are entitled to because the paperwork is complex and the process is opaque. A simple, phone-based service that takes a farmer's crop, location, and financial profile and tells him exactly which schemes he qualifies for, how to apply, and what documents he needs — and then follows up until the application is approved — would unlock hundreds of crores of government money that currently goes unspent. This is a software problem with a clear commercial model: a small success fee on each approved application.

• • •

THE CLOSING

I was building the platform I have described. Looking for joint venture partners who see the opportunity. Looking for investors who understand that this is not just profitable — it is necessary. Looking for AgriTech companies who want to add forward price intelligence to their existing offerings. Looking for entrepreneurs who want to solve this problem at scale.

Because the alternative is what I saw that morning at five am. My neighbour, who works harder than I ever have, earning a fraction of what his labour is worth, with a phone in his pocket that could change his life, and no idea that the opportunity exists.

That silence — that organised, institutional absence of anyone taking responsibility to inform, train, and equip the six hundred million people who feed this country — is unacceptable to me.

It should be unacceptable to you.

• • •

The man in the field will wake up at four tomorrow morning. He will milk his animals. He will look at what his neighbour is planting. He will make the same bet he has always made, with the same hope, the same uncertainty, and the same vulnerability.

Unless someone decides to change that.

The water is not coming. For agriculture, for the farmer, for the six hundred million people dependent on it, the wave is already here. Machines are replacing labour. Urban entrepreneurs are capturing the premium markets. Technology is transforming agriculture — but only for those who have access to it.

The question is not whether this will happen. It is happening. The question is: who gets to benefit? Who gets trained? Who gets equipped? Who gets included in the future, and who gets left behind to watch it happen to them?

That is still an open question.

And you have a role in the answer.

• • •

From the field at sunrise, where six hundred million people hold their breath and hope, I need to take you somewhere else now. Somewhere with air conditioning and fluorescent lights and rules about uniforms and productivity. Somewhere that also faces the same wave, with the same lack of warning, but in a very different form.

Come with me to the garment factory.

• • •

CHAPTER 3

THE SHIRT THAT NEVER FIT

FROM YOUR FRUSTRATION TO HER UNEMPLOYMENT.

Let me ask you something personal. When was the last time you bought a shirt that fit you perfectly? Not almost fit. Not fit-after-the-tailor-fixes-it. Perfectly. Off the rack, into the trial room, onto your body, and you looked in that mirror and thought: yes. This was made for me.

I will tell you my problem. I have long arms. Above average. If I find a shirt that fits my neck and shoulders, the sleeves stop short of my wrists. Every time. I have spent my entire adult life buying shirts that fit me in three places and betray me in one.

I was in a trial room recently, holding up a shirt that fit beautifully at the shoulders and ended an inch above my wrist, and I thought: who designed this? Who decided that this was a finished garment? And then I remembered. Nobody designed it for me. It was designed for soldiers.

In the 1860s, the American Civil War posed a problem no army had faced at scale before: how do you dress a million men quickly? There are no tailors. There is no time. So the manufacturers measured a few hundred soldiers, averaged the numbers, and built uniforms for four imaginary bodies — Small, Medium, Large, Extra Large. It worked well enough. A sleeve an inch short never stopped a bullet. Speed mattered. Fit did not.

The war ended. The sizing system did not. It moved from military camps into the factories of the industrial age because the factory had the same problem the army did: it needed to produce at speed, for bodies it would never meet. Four imaginary sizes became six, then eight, then slim fit and regular fit, and comfort fit. But the principle never changed.

The shirt was never designed to fit you. It was designed to fit the factory.

Now look around you. Look at the men in any Indian office, any wedding, any railway station. The man with the generous belly — his shirt is so tight the buttons are holding on for dear life, or so loose it hangs from his shoulders like a tent. There is no shirt on any rack in any showroom in this country designed for the actual shape of his body. You know this. You live with this. Every one of you reading this has walked out of a trial room with the option that was least wrong.

You have never questioned it because you have never imagined an alternative.

The alternative has arrived.

• • •

YOUR PHONE BECOMES YOUR TAILOR

Pick up your phone. Stand in front of a plain wall. Two photographs — front and side, fully clothed, thirty seconds.

An AI system can now extract over eighty precise measurements from those two images. Not just the chest and waist. The slope of your shoulders — because no two people's shoulders slope at the same angle. Your arm's length from shoulder to wrist. The precise distance from your collar to the natural break of your waist. Eighty measurements, accurate to within a few millimetres — more precise than any tailor who measures eight points and estimates the rest. A company called 3DLOOK does this today. From a phone camera. No booth. No appointment.

Now imagine what comes next. You open an app. It has your body — a three-dimensional shape of you, exactly. It has also studied your twenty favourite shirts: the colours you choose, the collar styles, the fits you actually wear, not what you claim to prefer in a survey. The AI knows you prefer structured shoulders and that you never buy checks smaller than half an inch. It shows you the shirts designed for your body — sleeves that reach your wrists, because the AI knows your arm length to the millimetre. You view the shirt on your digital avatar, rotating it. You change the fabric and press order.

Somewhere, a machine receives your unique pattern. An AI precisely arranged your pieces on fabric, wasting less than two percent. Humans, even cutting masters, waste fifteen to twenty-five percent when they cut by hand. A laser cuts your pieces. A robotic system assembles them.

Three to five days later, the shirt arrives.

It fits. Not almost. Not after the tailor. It fits because it was made for you — for the first time in the two-hundred-year history of mass-produced clothing.

You will never buy S, M, L, XL again.

• • •

WHY THIS IS NOT A FANTASY

I know what you are thinking. Technology conference. Rich people congratulating each other. Let me give you a number.

In 2024, the global fashion industry had approximately eight hundred and ninety billion dollars worth of clothing returned by customers. Seventy percent of those returns were because of fit. Eighty percent of the returned garments ended up in landfills or were burned. We are making billions of garments, shipping them across oceans, receiving a quarter back, and setting them on fire. We call this a functioning industry.

The mathematics of on-demand, made-to-measure manufacturing are, once you account for returns, unsold inventory, end-of-season markdowns, and destruction, already competitive with mass production. Amazon saw this years ago. They hold a patent for a fully automated clothing facility — a customer order triggers fabric printing, cutting, assembly, quality check, and shipping, with no human hand touching the garment. They are not pursuing this because it is interesting. They are pursuing it because the numbers are irresistible.

This is not ten years away. The technology exists. The economics are closing. The only question is the speed.

• • •

NOW THINK ABOUT HER

I have spent the last few pages making you excited. I meant every word. And now I need you to hold that excitement in one hand and hold something else in the other.

In Tirupur, Tamil Nadu, an alarm goes off at four in the morning. The room is small and the walls are close. Two families share it — her family on one side, her sister's on the other. The children sleep on the same mat. When the alarm sounds, it wakes everyone, and no one complains because this is how it is. She dresses without turning on the light. Ties her hair in the dark. She is out of the door before five because the walk to the factory takes forty minutes and the first bell is at six. Her name does not matter for this chapter, because she is not one woman. She is six hundred thousand women in Tirupur alone. She earns between eight and twelve thousand rupees a month. In some months, less. She has no union — fewer than four percent of Indian garment workers belong to one. She has no savings beyond what will carry her family through a week of missed wages. One illness, one delayed payment, one slow season at the factory, and the buffer is gone.

She sits at her station on the sewing line. Thirty machines in a row. She operates one of them. She does not make a shirt. She makes one part of a shirt, the left sleeve. That is her job. The motion is always the same: pick up the cut piece, align it under the needle, guide it through, cut the thread, place it in the pile, pick up the next piece. Her hands have done this so many times that they no longer wait for instructions from her mind. By afternoon, her fingers know the next piece before she reaches for it.

She attaches the left sleeve five hundred times today. As she did yesterday. As she will tomorrow. By the time she walks home, the light is gone. Her hands ache in the specific way that comes from ten thousand small, precise movements — not the ache of lifting or carrying but a deeper tightness in the tendons, a stiffness in the joints that she has had for so long she no longer notices it.

She does not know what a Sewbot is. She has never heard of 3DLOOK. Does not know that in a facility in the United States, a robotic sewing system can produce one million t-shirts a year on a single lease. Her entire line — thirty women — produces one hundred and fifty to one hundred and eighty thousand garments in that same year.

One machine. One million shirts. Thirty women. One hundred and eighty thousand shirts.

I will not insult you by pretending the mathematics are complicated.

But the Sewbot is the obvious threat. The one you can point to. What is more dangerous is what I described earlier — the phone scan, the digital twin, the shirt made specifically for one body in a facility three miles from the customer. Because that does not just replace her. It replaces the entire chain she lives inside.

The chain looks like this: a brand in New York orders fifty thousand identical shirts from a factory in Tirupur. The factory cuts, stitches, packs, and ships across an ocean. Some shirts get returned. Few sit unsold. Some are burned. But enough sell that the system remains profitable for everyone — except the woman on the sewing line, who earns eight thousand rupees regardless of how many shirts sell and how many burn.

Now imagine the future I described. The customer in New York scans his body on his phone, orders a shirt designed for him, and it is assembled in Ohio and delivered in three days. No ocean crossing. No Indian factory. No sewing line. No woman stitching the left sleeve five hundred times.

Every link in the chain is eliminated. Not disrupted. Eliminated. And not through malice; the customer simply wanted a shirt that fit. The technology company simply wanted to solve waste. The automated factory simply wanted to be efficient. Every actor made a rational choice. The cumulative effect is that forty-five million Indian garment workers are on ground that is running out from under them, without knowing it.

The old system's thread has almost run out. She is still stitching. No one has told her.

• • •

THE ACCELERANT NO ONE EXPECTED

If you have read the news in the past year, you know that the United States imposed a fifty percent tariff on Indian goods in 2025. The impact on Tirupur was immediate. Orders from American brands stopped overnight. In Tamil Nadu alone, three million jobs were threatened. Twenty thousand factories faced closure.

They negotiated the tariff down to eighteen percent in early 2026. The industry exhaled. Workers returned. And everyone treated it as a crisis survived.

It was not a crisis survived. It was a preview.

Because the question the tariff forced every American brand to ask was: why are we importing this at all?

The answer has always been labour cost. An Indian garment worker earns in a month what an American worker earns in a day. Thirty times cheaper. That gap is why shirts are stitched in Tirupur and worn in Texas. The tariff tried to close that gap through policy. It was clumsy, slow, and it hurt the poorest workers the most.

Automation closes the same gap through technology — permanently. A Sewbot does not earn thirty times less than an American worker. It does not earn at all. Runs twenty-four hours a day. It does not need housing, transport, or a provident fund. When the robot makes the shirt, there is no labour cost difference between Ohio and Tirupur. Zero. At that point, why ship a shirt across an ocean? Why accept the risk of a fifty percent tariff arriving overnight?

The tariff crisis of 2025 did not destroy India's garment exports. But it showed every global brand what life without Indian imports felt like — and it sped up their investment in the automation that will make those imports permanently unnecessary.

> *The Indian garment export industry exists for one reason: Indian hands are cheap. The moment machines become cheaper than cheap hands — and that moment is approaching — the reason vanishes. No trade agreement, no government scheme will change the arithmetic. You cannot compete with a cost of zero.*

EVEN THE COTTON

I can hear the optimist in you: fine, the stitching goes to machines, but India will always have cotton. India is the world's largest cotton producer. The raw material advantage stays.

A company called GALY, based in Boston, is growing real cotton in a laboratory. Not synthetic cotton. Not a cotton substitute. Actual cotton — from real plant cells, in steel bioreactors, year-round, independent of monsoons, independent of pesticides, using ninety-nine percent less water than field cotton.

Their investors include Bill Gates. Sam Altman, the man behind ChatGPT. H&M. And Inditex, the parent company of Zara.

Read that list again. The two most powerful names in artificial intelligence. The two most powerful names in fast fashion. Investing together in cotton grown without a farm.

In Japan, a company called Spiber uses fermentation — not unlike brewing beer — to create protein fibres that mimic silk, cashmere, and wool. They have a commercial factory in Thailand producing five hundred tonnes a year. Burberry has made scarves from it. The North Face has made jackets.

These are not conference presentations. They are products on shelves, backed by capital from people who do not invest in things that will not scale.

If cotton grows in a bioreactor in Ohio, India's cotton advantage disappears. If silk-like fibre brews in Thailand, India's silk heritage becomes a tourist attraction, not an economic engine. The countries investing in these technologies — America, Japan, Britain, the Netherlands — currently import textiles. They are not trying to beat India at India's game. They are cutting a new pattern entirely.

• • •

THE WOMAN WHO WILL NOT BECOME THE ROBOT TECHNICIAN

Every conversation about automation in Indian garments eventually offers the same reassurance: yes, these jobs will go, but new jobs will be created. Robot maintenance. Technical roles. Skilled positions in automated facilities.

This reassurance ignores one fact that anyone who has spent time in a Tirupur factory already knows: the garment workforce is predominantly female. The woman at the sewing machine in Bengaluru, the woman attaching the left sleeve in Tirupur; the woman checking fabric quality in Delhi-NCR — the repetitive, production-floor work of Indian garments is largely women's work. Often the sole income of the household. Often the first formal employment these women or their mothers have ever held.

The robot technician, the systems operator, the AI quality-control engineer who replaces the rows of women doing visual inspection — look at who fills those roles when Indian factories automate. They come from ITI diploma programmes, from engineering colleges, from the technical training pipeline. That pipeline is predominantly male.

This is not a conspiracy. It is the shape of every Indian industrial transition so far. New technology arrives, creates technical roles, and the technical roles go to people with technical training. The women who did the manual work that was replaced are rarely in that pipeline. They are too old to start. They have children. The training is in another city. The course takes six months they cannot afford.

So she does not become the robot technician. She goes home. Or she looks for the next available repetitive manual work — and finds that the wave is already arriving there too.

When we talk about forty-five million garment workers facing displacement, we are talking disproportionately about women. Women who are the primary earners in their households. Who have few alternative skills because the system never offered them any. Women who live in towns where the garment factory was the only formal employment on offer.

Reports about India's garment export ambitions almost never discuss this dimension of the disruption. This book must discuss this, because the uncle who refuses to let you sleep through a crisis also refuses to let you look away from who specifically gets hurt.

• • •

THREE WAVES

Let me be precise, because false urgency destroys credibility, and I am not interested in scaring you with a timeline I do not believe. This disruption is not one event. It is three waves, arriving at different speeds.

The first wave is already here. Organised Indian factories have automated their cutting rooms. Where a hundred and fifty workers once spread and cut fabric by hand, ten or twelve now operate machines. AI quality-inspection systems are replacing rows of women checking every seam with their eyes. Automated embroidery, printing, and packing are eliminating workers at the front and back of the production line. This wave is already affecting twelve to fifteen million workers across the textile chain — and most of them do not know why their shifts are getting shorter and their overtime is vanishing.

The second wave is three to seven years away. Robotic sewing reaches cost parity with Indian labour for basic garments — t-shirts, undergarments, simple stitching. Robot costs are falling fifteen to twenty percent per year. Indian wages are rising five percent. The lines will cross. When they do, the factory owner in Tirupur faces a choice that is not really a choice: automate or lose every export order to a competitor who did. This wave will displace another eight to twelve million workers. It will be visible, and it will be painful.

The third wave is a decade away, perhaps longer. This is what I have been describing in this chapter — the complete reimagining of how clothes are made and sold. Body scanning. AI design. On-demand manufacturing in consumer countries. Bio-engineered raw materials. This wave does not displace the sewing line. It eliminates the reason for the sewing line to be in India at all. Every technology I have described exists today, at some scale. The question is not whether they will converge. They will. The question is whether forty-five million people will be ready when they do.

• • •

THE PARADOX NOBODY IS TALKING ABOUT

The Government of India is building PM MITRA parks — mega integrated textile manufacturing clusters designed to make Indian garments globally competitive. The promise is compelling: world-class infrastructure, plug-and-play facilities, scale that smaller factories cannot achieve. This scheme has real money behind it and real ambition.

And it contains a contradiction that no one in the industry's public conversations will name.

A PM MITRA park that achieves global competitiveness will be an automated park. At a global scale, with global buyers demanding faster turnaround and lower prices every season, you do not compete with human labour at eight thousand rupees a month. You compete with machines. The brands that source from a PM MITRA park in 2030 will be the brands already investing in automation. They will expect it. They will require it.

The same scheme promises to create mass employment in Indian garments and simultaneously build the infrastructure for efficient automation deployment. The two goals — global competitiveness and mass employment — are on a collision course. Not in twenty years. In this decade.

Nobody in the official conversation about PM MITRA is saying this. Industry associations are celebrating the infrastructure. The government is celebrating the investment. The workers who will one day find themselves inside these modern, efficient, increasingly automated facilities have not been part of any conversation at all.

The uncle is not angry with the scheme. Infrastructure investment is real and necessary. The uncle is angry at the silence — the complete absence of any plan for what happens to the workers when the competitive pressure that these parks are designed to survive turns, as competitive pressure always does, into the pressure to automate.

• • •

WHAT COULD BE BUILT?

Every chapter in this book ends with ideas for entrepreneurs — not prescriptions, not guaranteed businesses, but clear gaps that someone with energy and clarity of purpose could fill. The garment sector has three that I find compelling.

The first is the portable credential. The garment worker has no formal record of her skills. She can stitch a left sleeve five hundred times a day with machine precision, but there is no document, no certificate, no verified record of this capability that travels with her. When the factory closes, she starts from scratch. A phone-based skills certification programme — taught in Tamil, in Telugu, in Hindi, in twenty-minute daily modules — that gives a garment worker a verifiable credential before she needs it, not after, is a business that addresses a real and urgent gap. The credential does not have to be for garment skills. It can be for adjacent skills — quality control, inventory management, logistics — that the automation wave needs, even as it displaces the sewing line.

The second is the worker-owned brand. AI design tools and direct-to-consumer digital channels now make it possible to build a clothing brand without the intermediary layers that have always extracted the margin between Tirupur and the customer. A cooperative of skilled tailors — owning the brand, owning the platform, using AI for design and body-fit technology, selling directly to the customer — captures the value that currently goes to the brand in New York and the platform in Mumbai. This model exists in other sectors. No one has seriously attempted it in Indian garments. It should be.

The third is the early warning system. Global fashion order flows are trackable. Automation investment announcements are public. Brand sourcing shift decisions leave detectable signals months before they become visible in factory order books. A platform that monitors these signals and gives garment clusters — workers, local governments, training organisations — two or three years of advance notice before displacement arrives is not a technology moonshot. It is an aggregation and analysis problem that a small, focused team could build. Two years of warning is the difference between a worker who retrained and a worker who is unemployed.

• • •

YOUR SHIRT AND HER HANDS

I want to end this chapter where I started it. With a shirt that does not fit.

The next time you stand in a trial room and feel the sleeve stop an inch short of your wrist, or see the fabric strain across your belly, or notice the shoulder seam sitting wrong — understand that you are feeling the last days of a two-hundred-year-old system. The discomfort is not a personal inconvenience. It is a symptom of a manufacturing model built for a nineteenth-century soldier that has run its course.

And when that system breaks — when technology finally delivers a garment made for your body — the relief you feel will be real. The fit will be perfect. The waste will be gone. Shopping will be, for the first time, what it should always have been.

But somewhere in Tirupur, a woman who woke before dawn, who walked forty minutes to sit at a machine, whose hands know the left sleeve the way yours know a phone number — she will walk home with her last pay packet. She will not know that your frustration with sleeve length funded the technology that replaced her. She will know only that the orders stopped, the factory closed, and the eight thousand rupees that kept her children in school are gone.

Your perfect shirt is her unemployment.

That is not a reason to stop progress. The pattern has been cut. It cannot be restitched into the old shape. But it is a reason — an urgent, moral, human reason — to demand that someone, somewhere, is preparing her for what comes after. Training her before the factory closes. Building the credential before the line stops. Creating the cooperative before she is desperate.

That someone must include the people reading this book.

• • •

CHAPTER 4

THE BOY ON THE BIKE

GIG WORKERS, DELIVERY PLATFORMS, AND THE BETRAYAL NOBODY ANNOUNCED

Let me tell you about Rajan.

He is twenty-three years old. He came from a small village in Bhojpur district, Bihar, three years ago. He had finished Class 12, which is more education than his father had. He had tried twice for a government job and not made it. He had spent six months working construction on a site in Patna, carrying bricks in the forty-degree heat, and decided he needed something better.

Someone told him: come to Delhi, download the app, get a second-hand bike, and you can earn twenty-five thousand rupees a month. Be your own boss. Choose your own hours. Nobody tells you what to do.

He came. He downloaded the app. He got the bike. He is now delivering food and groceries across a three-kilometre radius of a Blinkit dark store in Gurgaon, ten to twelve hours a day, six days a week. His earnings last month were fourteen thousand rupees. From that, he pays two thousand for a shared room and approximately three thousand in fuel and bike maintenance. He sends six thousand home. He keeps three thousand to live on.

He is not his own boss. He has never been his own boss. He has an algorithm for a boss — one that assigns him orders, times his deliveries, penalises him when traffic makes him late, and can deactivate his ID without warning and without appeal. He has no union, no pension, no health insurance, no severance. He is classified as a 'delivery partner,' which sounds warm and collaborative and means, in law, exactly nothing.

He does not know that the platform that gave him this work is simultaneously, right now, testing the drones and robots that will make his bike and his body unnecessary.

Nobody told him.

• • •

Rajan is not unusual. He is the median. He is the face of twelve million people who make up India's gig delivery workforce today — and twenty-three and a half million by 2030, if the government's projections are correct. He is the boy on the bike that every Indian has seen from their balcony or their car window: the helmet, the thermal bag on his back, the phone on the handlebar, navigating the gap between two trucks at a speed that makes you wince.

He is the most modern-looking worker in India's economy. He uses GPS. He processes digital payments. He is connected to the city's nervous system in real time. He is also, in the framework of this book, exactly as vulnerable as the liftman who pressed the elevator button. His repetition cycle — accept order, navigate to restaurant, pick up food, navigate to address, deliver, return, accept next order — runs dozens of times per shift. The same loop, managed by machine, building toward the moment the machine decides it no longer needs him to close it.

• • •

WHAT I SEE FROM MY BUILDING WINDOW

I want to tell you what I see every time I order something to my building in Mumbai.

The delivery boy arrives. He cannot park his bike in the building compound. Our society rules do not permit it. In many buildings, residents have specifically banned delivery workers from using the lifts, directing them to service stairs or back entrances that may or may not actually exist. So he parks on the street, blocking part of the lane. And the watchman at the gate — the same man I wrote about in Chapter One, whose own post is being quietly automated away — comes out and argues with him about the motorcycle. The delivery boy argues back, one eye on the app timer, knowing every extra minute is burning his rating. The argument is pointless because neither man made the rules and neither man has any power to change them.

Then he runs. Up the stairs if the lift is denied. Through the lobby if it is not. To the door. The resident takes the bag, says thank you. The delivery boy is already turning, already checking the phone, because the next order has been assigned.

I stand at my door and think: we built a system that sends this young man to serve the building residents, and we could not agree to give him somewhere to park his bike.

Think about what we do for other service providers. A doctor visits a residential complex and there is reserved parking. A generator technician arrives and the building makes space. But the delivery worker, who comes fifty times a day to the same building bringing food and medicine and groceries for the people who live there, is left to argue at the gate about where his motorcycle is standing.

The solution is not complicated. Mark a delivery bay near the entrance. Give each delivery worker temporary access for the three minutes it takes to complete a job. This requires no legislation, no technology, no government scheme. It requires a building committee to spend twenty minutes deciding to be decent. The absence of that solution tells you exactly how we see these workers. They are service infrastructure, like the electricity cable or the water pipe. They come in through the back. They are invisible when things run smoothly and inconvenient when they do not. They are not people whose time or safety or dignity we have thought to plan for.

I watch them at traffic signals. The light turns amber and the delivery boy accelerates, not slows. Because decelerating costs him seconds. Seconds cost him his rating. His rating controls his income. He is not reckless by nature. The system made him reckless by design.

• • •

The platform economy arrived in India as a revolution in how ordinary people could earn a living. Swiggy and Zomato were celebrated in the press as job creators. In a country where formal employment is scarce and the alternatives are construction labour, domestic work, or the farm — all backbreaking, all underpaid — here was something different. A smartphone, a bike, a small registration fee, and you were a 'delivery partner.' The language was carefully chosen. Not employee. Not labourer. Partner. The word carried a promise of equality, of agency, of entrepreneurship.

And in the early days, the earnings were real. Workers who joined Swiggy and Zomato in 2016 and 2017 report earning twenty to twenty-five thousand rupees a month. The platforms were burning investor money to acquire market share, paying high rates to attract riders, offering sign-on bonuses, fuel subsidies, incentive schemes. The ecosystem felt generous.

What was actually happening is a pattern used in every platform economy in the world, from Uber in San Francisco to Deliveroo in London. The platforms use investor capital to subsidise the early experience — for consumers and workers both. Prices are low, rates are high, the product feels miraculous. Users become dependent. Workers build their lives around the income. And then, once the habit is established and the dependency is locked in, the rate cards begin to fall.

A 2022 study by the National Council of Applied Economic Research found that the real wages of gig workers had fallen eleven percent since 2019, dropping to an average of eleven thousand nine hundred and sixty-three rupees per month even before expenses. A 2024 study found that forty-three percent of delivery workers earn under ten thousand rupees per month. The forty-one-year-old Swiggy driver in Hyderabad who spoke to CNN on the night of the New Year's Eve strike said his base rate was five rupees per order. Five rupees. Less than a cup of tea at the dhaba next to his dark store. He works from 7pm to 5am every day. He makes it work through volume — enough deliveries, enough hours, enough suppression of the thought that there might be a better way to live.

A policy researcher who has studied South Asia's gig economy described it precisely: the language of being your own boss attracted people at first, but what the gig economy has essentially done is formalise the informalisation of workers. The informality of the village — no contract, no certainty, no safety net — was brought inside a corporate app and called the future of work.

That is the first betrayal. The second is still being built in drone testing facilities and robotic fulfilment centres across the country. The platforms are quietly building the technology that will make even this informal arrangement unnecessary. The first betrayal convinced workers they were entrepreneurs. The second will tell them they are obsolete.

• • •

THE ALGORITHM IS YOUR BOSS – AND IT CANNOT BE REASONED WITH

Here is what being managed by an algorithm actually means in practice.

Your income is not a salary. It is the output of a formula you cannot see, negotiating variables you cannot control. Which orders you receive, how far they are, whether there is a surge bonus active right now, whether your rating is high enough to qualify for today's incentive — all of this is determined by software. The formula changes. The rate card changes. The incentive structure changes. You find out when your earnings are lower than you expected at the end of the day.

Your rating determines your income. Customers rate every delivery on a scale that they do not fully understand, and their ratings feed an algorithm that does not distinguish between a bad delivery and a bad mood. A customer who is unhappy about their food — food that was prepared by the restaurant, not by Rajan — rates the delivery two stars. Rajan's rating drops. His access to better orders shrinks. His income falls.

His ID can be deactivated without warning. No hearing. No appeal. No explanation beyond a notification that his account has been suspended pending review. He has no HR department to call. No union to represent him. No law that requires the platform to give him a reason.

This is not a design flaw. It is a design choice. The algorithm is the boss precisely because an algorithmic boss cannot be negotiated with, cannot be embarrassed, and does not need to justify itself. The informality that feels like freedom is actually a precision tool for removing every form of worker leverage.

• • •

THE COST OF TEN MINUTES

On his first day as a delivery worker in Delhi, eighteen-year-old Ankush from Bihar was killed in a road accident. He had just arrived from his village. He had completed the onboarding. He had his bike. He was on his first shift. He was eighteen years old.

The government issued an advisory to platforms to review ten-minute delivery targets. There was no enforcement mechanism. The platforms continued.

On New Year's Eve, the night between 2025 and 2026, more than two hundred thousand delivery workers went on strike across every major city simultaneously — Swiggy, Zomato, Blinkit, Amazon, Flipkart, Zepto. Their demands were the same things they had been asking for years: fair pay, an end to the ten-minute death trap, accident insurance, pensions, basic dignity.

Deepinder Goyal, the founder of Zomato and Blinkit, posted on X that both platforms had delivered at a record pace, unaffected by calls for strikes, and that local law enforcement had been helpful in keeping 'miscreants' in check.

The Telangana Gig and Platform Workers Union responded that seven and a half million orders were delivered that night — because workers cannot afford to log out, not because the system treats them justly.

Both statements are true. That is what makes this so hard to look at directly.

• • •

HE IS TRAINING HIS OWN REPLACEMENT

Now I need to tell you something about Rajan's bike that he does not know.

Every trip he makes is being recorded. Not just for quality assurance. Not just to verify the delivery happened. Every route he takes, every shortcut he has discovered, every traffic pattern he has learned to read — the time of day when the road outside the apartment complex is clear, the lane that moves fastest near the school during pickup hour, the building whose watchman will let him park inside so he saves two minutes — all of this data is being harvested by the platform.

It is being used to train the navigation system that will eventually guide an autonomous delivery robot through the same streets. Rajan's three years of local knowledge, accumulated at personal risk, through near-misses in traffic and wrong turns on dark nights — this is the raw material from which the platform is building his replacement.

He is doing this for free. He is paying for the fuel himself.

This is not a conspiracy. Nobody sat in a boardroom and said: let us trick these men into training their own replacements. The data collection is simply what platforms do — it makes the service better, which is what platforms are built to do. The fact that 'better service' will eventually mean 'no human in the loop' is not something anyone is obligated to announce. There is no law that says a platform must tell its workers it is investing in the technology that will make them redundant.

There is also no law that says they must not.

He is, unknowingly, training his own replacement. The most modern-looking worker in India's economy is doing the most vulnerable job in it.

• • •

WHAT IS ACTUALLY BEING BUILT

Let me be precise about the automation timeline, because false urgency destroys credibility and I am not interested in alarming you with things I do not believe.

The warehouse has already changed. This is not three to seven years away. It is happening now.

Inside the fulfilment centres of Amazon, Flipkart, and Delhivery, robots built by Indian companies are already sorting, picking, and moving packages. Addverb Technologies, Unbox Robotics, and GreyOrange — all Indian or India-operating — deploy robotic systems that process thousands of packages per hour. A robotic sorter processes packages in under three seconds. A human sorter, working at full pace, takes eight to ten. The robot does not take lunch. It does not call in sick. It does not ask for a provident fund contribution.

Amazon's own internal documents, leaked in late 2025, revealed a plan to reduce the need for six hundred thousand warehouse workers globally by 2033 — driven by its next-generation robots, including a system called Vulcan, which now has a sense of touch delicate enough to handle fragile packages that previously required human hands. The company said publicly that those documents represented 'one team's view.' The investment trajectory — over sixty billion dollars in robotics and automation capital expenditure — suggests otherwise.

The workers sorting and packing parcels in Indian warehouses have a repetition cycle measured in seconds. They are first.

The dark store — the small neighbourhood warehouse from which Blinkit and Zepto fulfil ten-minute orders — is next. A human picker running through a dark store, selecting items from shelves, takes forty to sixty seconds per item on average. A robotic system takes eight to twelve. The dark store robot does not need to be paid between orders. It does not call the union when its schedule changes.

The drone is three to seven years away at scale. This needs to be said carefully because drone delivery is easy to mock — it has been 'three years away' for the past decade. But the economics are now genuinely moving. Today, last-mile delivery by a human rider on a petrol scooter costs approximately ten rupees per kilometre. Drone delivery currently costs around one hundred rupees per kilometre — ten times more. This is why it has not scaled

But there are Indian startups redesigning drones from first principles, not iterating on existing models. Airbound is the most interesting of them. Their target is thirty paise per kilometre. Not ten rupees. Not one rupee. Thirty paise. If that engineering succeeds — and the physics do not rule it out — the economics of last-mile delivery in Indian cities will change irreversibly. A drone that costs thirty paise per kilometre does not call in sick. It does not have a family in Bihar it needs to send money to. It does not run amber lights because the algorithm is threatening its rating.

Serious people in India's drone logistics sector are talking about a window of five to eight years for urban gated community delivery. For open urban environments, a decade. The delivery boy has between five and ten years before his loop closes.

• • •

THE TRUCK DRIVER: A DIFFERENT TIMELINE

Before I leave the road entirely, I want to take you to a different one.

The National Highways of India. The Delhi-Mumbai Expressway. The six-lane corridors that have transformed how goods move across this country.

There are approximately nine million truck drivers in India. They are a different kind of worker from the delivery boy — older, more experienced, often owner-operators who have their own vehicle, often members of cooperatives, often from families where driving a truck is a generational occupation. They have been the invisible engine of India's economic growth for decades. Every product in every store arrived on a truck. Every raw material in every factory came on a truck.

The truck driver's repetition cycle is longer than the delivery boy's. His route requires genuine skill — reading other drivers, managing fatigue, navigating diverse road conditions, dealing with checkposts and dhaba timings and the arithmetic of permits and overload penalties. This is not a simple loop.

Autonomous trucks will eventually come to Indian highways. But eventually is the honest word here. The timeline for full autonomous trucking on Indian roads — with their cattle crossings, their counterflow traffic, their unmapped villages, their infinite variety of chaos — is long. Engineers working at Indian-specific autonomous vehicle companies like Minus Zero and Flux Auto are careful about this. They know what the American timeline looked like even on well-marked, well-maintained, low-chaos American highways: it has taken longer than anyone predicted.

The truck driver will not be automated in five years. He probably will not be fully automated in ten. What will happen — and is already beginning — is compression. Semi-autonomous systems on expressways allow one lead driver to manage a convoy of three or four trucks, the following trucks running autonomously in highway conditions. Three drivers become one. Across nine million truck drivers, a thirty percent reduction in demand over fifteen years is close to three million people looking for other work. In a country where other work is already scarce.

I am not adding truck drivers to the urgent alarm in this chapter. Their timeline is different. But I want you to have seen them. No chapter on logistics is complete without the man who has been doing this the longest, who will be disrupted last, who everyone will forget about until the disruption arrives.

• • •

WHAT THE LAW DOES AND DOES NOT DO

India's governments have begun to notice. Slowly. Partially. Too late for the workers already in the system, but not too late for those who have not yet joined.

Rajasthan became the first state in India to pass a law protecting gig workers in July 2023. The Rajasthan Platform Based Gig Workers (Registration and Welfare) Act requires platforms to register every worker with a unique ID, creates a welfare fund financed by a cess on every platform transaction, and establishes a board to oversee social security benefits including health insurance, accident coverage, and pension contributions. By August 2025, Karnataka, Bihar, and Jharkhand had passed similar legislation. Telangana released a draft bill. Several other states are watching.

This is genuine progress. Workers who are registered, who have a unique ID that travels with them across platforms, who have access to accident insurance — these workers are less vulnerable than the workers who had none of that. The legislative movement is real and it matters.

But here is what the legislation does not do.

It does not reclassify gig workers as employees. They remain contractors. The fundamental asymmetry — platform bears no obligation to provide work, worker bears full risk of income volatility — remains intact. It does not address algorithmic management. The rating system that can destroy a worker's income based on a customer's mood, the ID deactivation with no appeal, the shifting rate cards — none of this is touched by the welfare boards.

And most critically: the legislation does not prepare these workers for the automation that will make the entire question of their welfare redundant. The welfare board is being set up to protect workers in a job category that the same economy is systematically building the tools to eliminate. It is building a safety net under a cliff that someone is about to bulldoze.

The question the legislation does not ask is the question this book exists to ask. If the platforms were always going to automate this workforce, why were they allowed to build this workforce without any obligation to retrain or protect the workers against displacement? The platforms used these twelve million people to build a habit in the Indian consumer, to map Indian cities, to train their own navigation systems — and now face no obligation to do anything for those workers when the robot arrives.

Who is responsible for that gap? And who will fill it?

• • •

WHAT COULD BE BUILT

The worker-owned platform cooperative is the cleanest solution and the hardest to build. The idea is simple: use the same technology stack as Swiggy and Zomato but structure the ownership so that the delivery workers are shareholders, not contractors. The margins that currently go to the platform go to the workers instead. The algorithmic management is governed by the workers who operate within it, not by executives who have never made a delivery in their lives.

This is not a fantasy. In France, a platform cooperative called CoopCycle provides technology to worker-owned delivery cooperatives in fifty European cities. In India, the taxi sector already has a working model: Namma Yatri in Karnataka, an app-based ride platform that operates without a middleman and returns the full fare to the driver. It processed ten million rides in its first year. It works. The entrepreneur who builds the Indian equivalent for food and grocery delivery will not become a billionaire. But they will build something with genuine value — a platform that gives workers ownership of what they helped create, that survives the automation wave longer because it is not spending its margins funding its own displacement.

The portable credential is the second opportunity. Today, Rajan's reliability rating, his delivery record, his customer scores — all of this lives inside Swiggy's system. If he switches to Zomato, he starts from zero. If he switches to Amazon, zero again. He cannot build a professional identity that crosses platform boundaries. The platform owns his reputation. A portable, verifiable gig worker credential — worker-owned, readable by any platform — would give workers something they currently do not have: a professional history that belongs to them. A worker with five years of clean delivery record and high customer satisfaction should be able to take that record anywhere, use it to access better insurance rates, negotiate better terms with platforms, and demonstrate reliability to any employer. This is a relatively simple technology problem. Government can mandate it. The entrepreneur who builds the neutral infrastructure first, before the mandate, will have significant advantage when the mandate arrives.

The third opportunity is the transition itself. When drones handle simple, standardised deliveries — the grocery order, the takeout box — what remains for human workers is the delivery that requires human judgment. Medical supplies to elderly residents who need to be checked on. High-value items that need a signature and a face-to-face handoff. Deliveries to locations that drones cannot reach — dense urban lanes, buildings with restricted access, addresses in areas that are not yet drone-mapped. The delivery worker retrained not as a generic courier but as a specialist in complex, high-touch last-mile delivery will find that his human qualities — judgment, empathy, the ability to handle unexpected situations — become more valuable, not less, as the simple loop is automated. He is paid more, he works fewer hours, and he delivers what the drone cannot. This is a genuine transition pathway. It requires training, it requires platform design that carves out this role deliberately, and it requires someone to build the bridge between where Rajan is today and where he could be when the wave hits.

THE CLOSE

I want to take you back to the morning of New Year's Day 2026. Two hundred thousand delivery workers had just walked off in the biggest labour action the gig economy had ever seen in India. Orders were still going out because workers could not afford to stop. Platforms declared the strike a failure. The news cycle moved on in forty-eight hours.

And somewhere in Gurgaon, Rajan got back on his bike.

Not because the system is fair. He knows it is not fair. Not because the situation had improved. It had not. But because the alternative — going back to the village, admitting the city had not worked out, watching his daughter's school fees fall behind — was worse. He got back on the bike because the bike is what he has.

That is the trap I need you to understand. The man on the bike is not ignorant. He is not passive. He is trapped between a present that is grinding him down and a future he cannot yet see. He cannot afford to stop long enough to prepare for what is coming. He is, right now, in the most dangerous position a person can be in during a technological disruption: too dependent on the current system to leave it, and too unwarned about the future system to prepare for it.

The wave that will displace him will not arrive in the dramatic form of a factory closing or an employer announcing layoffs. It will arrive quietly, as these waves always do. First the warehouse workers. Then the dark store pickers. Then the simple, standardised deliveries. Then the groceries. By the time the displacement is visible enough to generate outrage, millions of people will already be out of the loop.

He deserves to be warned. He deserves to be trained. He deserves a system that acknowledges his contribution to the economy he helped build — the maps he drew, the routes he optimised, the data he generated — and treats that contribution as a reason to invest in his future, not a resource to extract and discard.

That is not a romantic notion. It is a practical one. A country with twelve million displaced workers and no alternative for them is not a stable country. The disruption described in this chapter is not a technology story. It is a social contract story. India built its quick commerce miracle on the backs of twelve million young men from Bihar and UP and Odisha. The question of what happens to those men when the miracle no longer needs their backs is the most important policy question in India's digital economy.

Nobody is asking it seriously yet.

Get back on the bike, Rajan. But when you do — know that the wave is there. Know that the time to prepare is now, not when the order stops coming. And know that there are people who see you, who understand what you have contributed, and who believe that you deserve better than to be a stepping stone that the economy crosses and forgets.

• • •

We have now visited the gate, the field, the factory floor, and the road. We have met the watchman whose building is automating around him, the farmer whose market is moving without him, the woman whose stitch is being replicated by a machine in Ohio, and the boy on the bike who is drawing the map of his own replacement.

In each sector, the same pattern. The technology exists. The economics are moving. The workers are unwarned. The silence is organised and institutional. And the consequences, when they arrive, will not stay in the sector where they begin. They will spill into the streets, into the cities, into the politics of a country that has not made peace with what it is about to become.

Come with me to the construction site.

• • •

CHAPTER 5

THE TRAP CLOSING FROM BOTH SIDES

CONSTRUCTION & INFRASTRUCTURE

THE MAN WHO LEFT THE FARM

Let me tell you about Ramesh.

He is forty-three years old. For twelve years, he has been working on construction sites in Pune. Before that, he was in his village in Uttar Pradesh, doing farm labour — the same work his father did, his grandfather did. Transplanting rice. Harvesting wheat. Two hundred and fifty rupees a day when there was work. Nothing when there was not.

Twelve years ago, he made a decision that felt like survival. He left.

His cousin told him there was construction work in the city. Buildings going up everywhere. Always need men to mix cement, carry bricks, tie rebar. The money was better — four hundred rupees a day, sometimes five hundred. Enough to send eight thousand rupees home every month. Enough for his son to stay in school. Enough to believe he had made the right choice.

Every morning, Ramesh wakes at five and walks from the labour colony — where he shares a room with three other men — to the construction site where a new apartment tower is rising. Thirty floors. Two years of work, the supervisor says. He has cycled through five different buildings over twelve years. The sites change. The work does not.

He sends money home. His son is in tenth standard now. Ramesh is proud of this. He believes his son will finish school, maybe even go to college, and never have to do what Ramesh does. He believes construction work will always exist because India will always be building. Every city he sees is full of cranes and half-finished towers. There will always be work for men willing to carry bricks.

Ramesh has never heard of a bricklaying robot. He has never heard of 3D-printed houses. He does not know that in China, they built a thirty-story building in fifteen days using prefabricated modules assembled like Lego blocks. He does not know that in Florida, a robot laid all the bricks for an entire house in a single day.

And here is what keeps me awake at night: Ramesh does not know that the village he left — where farm work was disappearing — now has rice transplanting machines that do the work of ten labourers. The choice he made twelve years ago, to leave the automated farm for the city construction site, was not an escape. It was moving from one side of a closing trap to the other.

The farm automated behind him. The construction site is automating in front of him.

• • •

SEVENTY MILLION PEOPLE – INDIA'S SECOND-LARGEST EMPLOYER

Construction employs seventy to seventy-one million workers in India today. This makes it the second-largest employer in the country, after agriculture. Not manufacturing. Not services. Not the celebrated technology sector. Construction.

The government projects one hundred million construction workers by 2030 — eight million new jobs added every year. Infrastructure spending is at historic highs. Roads, metros, airports, smart cities, housing — the building boom is real. The cranes are everywhere. The projects are massive.

And yet — and this is the paradox that makes this sector so dangerous — growth and displacement are happening simultaneously.

The projection of one hundred million workers assumes we keep building the way we have always built. It assumes that every tower, every highway, every metro line will be constructed the same way Ramesh's grandfather would recognise: humans mixing cement by hand, humans carrying bricks on their heads, humans tying rebar with their fingers. But that assumption is already breaking. Quietly. Site by site. Task by task.

The primary source states are Uttar Pradesh, Bihar, Odisha, Rajasthan, Madhya Pradesh. Read that list again. These are the same states that supply security guards. The same states that supply agricultural labourers. The same states that supply garment workers and delivery boys. When work disappears in the village, young men migrate to the city. When they arrive, they find construction.

Construction is the economic safety valve for rural unemployment. It absorbs the millions who cannot survive on the farm. It has done this for decades. It was Ramesh's escape route twelve years ago. It is the escape route for hundreds of thousands of young men every year.

But an escape route only works if there is somewhere to escape to. And that is the question this chapter forces you to confront: when the farm has automated and the city construction site is automating, where does Ramesh's son go?

• • •

THE REPETITION CYCLE: LIFT, PLACE, REPEAT

Ramesh arrives at the site at six. The morning begins with his body, not his mind. Twelve years have made these motions automatic. He does not decide to mix cement the way you decide to write an email. His arms move before the thought forms.

Morning: Mixing Cement.

A pile of sand. A pile of cement powder. Water from a hose. He uses a shovel. Shovel the sand. Shovel the cement. Add water. Mix. The motion is a full rotation of the spine — bend forward, scoop, rotate, pour — repeated several hundred times in two hours. His lower back carries the debt of twelve years of this. He knows precisely how long he can go before the pain becomes an instruction to stop.

A concrete batching plant — a machine that costs twenty to thirty lakh rupees — mixes cement continuously, precisely, without a human touching a shovel. The mix is consistent. The output is five times faster. The machine does not accumulate a twelve-year debt in its lower back. Automated batching plants in Indian precast factories are already reducing dependency on manual labour. Ramesh's morning task is being eliminated in organised construction. Not tomorrow. Now.

Midday: Carrying Bricks.

After the cement is mixed, Ramesh carries bricks. They arrive on trucks. He and five other men load them onto wooden planks and carry the planks up bamboo scaffolding to the floor where the mason is working. Twenty bricks per load. Fifty kilograms. Twelve trips per hour. The scaffolding sways slightly under their weight. Nobody discusses this.

A material hoist — a motorised elevator system — carries five hundred kilograms of bricks to any floor in three minutes. One operator manages the hoist. The six men carrying bricks are no longer needed. But even the hoist is becoming outdated. In prefabricated construction, bricks never come to the site loose. The walls arrive pre-assembled in panels, lifted by crane, bolted into place. No bricks to carry. No scaffolding to climb. No Ramesh.

Afternoon: Tying Rebar.

Steel rods laid in a grid, tied together with wire at every intersection to form the skeleton that will hold the concrete. Ramesh uses a small hook tool. Wrap the wire. Twist. Pull tight. Move to the next intersection. Eight hundred to a thousand times in an afternoon. His hands cramp in a particular way by three o'clock — the fingers curling inward even when he is not holding the tool. This is what twelve years of tying wire does to a hand.

Vision-equipped robots now automate rebar tying, improving structural strength and removing the human cost of this task entirely. These robots are commercially available. They tie faster, more consistently, and they will never develop the three o'clock cramp.

What is Ramesh's repetition cycle? Lift the brick. Place the brick. Bend and mix. Tie the wire. Repeat. His cycle is measured in seconds. In the framework of this book, he is standing at the edge of a cliff. And unlike the security guard or the garment worker, Ramesh does not even know there is a cliff. He believes construction is immune to automation because buildings are physical. Because cement is heavy. Because someone has to be there to do the work.

He is wrong.

• • •

THIS IS NOT ABOUT CRANES REPLACING PULLEYS

We have always mechanised construction. A crane replaced a hundred men with ropes pulling stones. A cement mixer replaced ten men with shovels. An excavator replaced fifty men with pick-axes. This is normal progress. Every industry mechanises. Construction has been mechanising for a century.

This is not that.

What follows is not mechanisation. It is the application of artificial intelligence to the entire construction process — from the moment you think "I want a building" to the moment you walk through the door. And AI does not just make the existing process faster. It makes the existing process obsolete.

• • •

FROM YOUR WORDS TO A FINISHED BUILDING IN FOUR MONTHS

You are a developer. You want to build a fifty-unit apartment building in Bangalore. You have the land. You need the design.

Twenty years ago, you would hire an architect. Meetings. Descriptions. Sketches. Feedback. Revisions. Months would pass. Fees would accumulate.

Today, you open an AI-powered architectural design platform. You type in plain language: "Fifty-unit apartment building, Bangalore, ten thousand square metre plot, maximise natural light, two-bedroom and three-bedroom units, budget-conscious materials, fast construction, modern aesthetic, comply with local building codes." The AI processes this in ninety seconds. It generates fifteen different design options. Complete floor plans. 3D renderings. Structural calculations. Cost estimates. Material lists. Construction timelines. All fifteen options are code-compliant, structurally sound, and optimised for the constraints you specified. You like Option 7 but want the balconies from Option 3 and the stairwell placement from Option 11. You tell the AI. It generates a new hybrid design in thirty seconds.

You have gone from idea to final architectural design in twenty minutes. The architect who would have spent three months on this project and charged fifteen lakh rupees has been replaced by a software subscription costing fifty thousand rupees per year.

But this is just the beginning.

The AI immediately analyses the design and breaks it down into components for factory manufacture — bathroom pods, kitchen modules, bedroom wall panels, precast staircases, balcony sections, electrical and plumbing assemblies, all pre-wired, pre-piped. It calculates which components should be 3D-printed, which assembled using robotic arms, which cast in traditional moulds. It optimises for fastest factory production time and easiest on-site assembly sequence. It generates the manufacturing instructions — the digital files that robots and 3D printers will read. An engineer would have taken two weeks. The AI did it in four minutes.

The digital files go to a prefabrication factory running twenty-four hours a day. A 3D concrete printer receives the file for bathroom pods. It prints one complete bathroom pod — walls, floor, ceiling, plumbing channels embedded during printing — in six hours. No bricklayer. No plasterer. No tile layer. Robotic arms in another section cut steel rebar to exact specifications, place it in moulds, pour concrete, vibrate it for compaction, cure it under controlled temperature. One robotic cell produces twenty wall panels per day. A human crew of twelve workers would produce five panels per day.

In six weeks, the entire building — broken into transportable modules — is manufactured in the factory. The traditional on-site construction timeline for the same building would be twelve months with one hundred workers on-site every day.

The modules arrive at the Bangalore site over two weeks. On-site, there is no army of workers mixing cement and tying rebar. There is a foundation poured in advance, a large crane, and fifteen technicians operating AI-powered assembly robots. The crane reads the digital blueprint. It knows which module goes where. It lifts a bathroom pod from the truck and positions it on the third floor, accurate to within five millimetres, in twelve minutes. Robotic welding arms secure it to the structural frame. Wall panels are bolted into place, alignment checked in real time by laser sensors. Kitchen modules are craned into position, connected to pre-installed plumbing and electrical risers. Staircases dropped in. Balconies attached.

In six weeks, the building is assembled. Weather delays: minimal — most work happened in the factory. Labour shortages: irrelevant — the factory runs on a fixed schedule. Quality issues: nearly zero — every component was manufactured under controlled conditions and inspected by AI before leaving the factory.

Total time from design prompt to finished building: four months. Total labour: fifteen factory technicians for six weeks. Fifteen on-site technicians for six weeks.

Compare this to traditional construction: twelve months. One hundred on-site workers. Unpredictable weather delays. Quality inconsistencies. Cost overruns.

Ramesh can carry bricks very well after twelve years of practice. But he cannot be retrained in three months to carry fifty different types of components, assembled in fifty different sequences, on fifty different projects. The robot can.

• • •

THE TECHNOLOGY THAT ALREADY EXISTS

Everything below is operational today, commercially available, and being deployed on construction sites around the world — including in India. The only question is how fast it spreads.

Bricklaying Robots.

Picture Ramesh standing next to the Hadrian X on a site in Florida. He lays fifty to sixty bricks an hour on a good day — more than most, after twelve years. The Hadrian X lays over three hundred blocks an hour. It does not slow in the afternoon heat. It does not take lunch. It worked through the night and by morning the entire brick structure of a full house was complete. One day. One robot. Walls up. Windows framed. Done.

The SAM100 bricklaying robot lays three thousand bricks daily. Ramesh and two other men, working a full day, might lay six hundred between them. The robot lays three thousand. Alone.

A building site employs ten bricklayers, each earning twenty-five thousand rupees per month. Add the supervisor's cut, the contractor's margin, the mandated ESI and PF contributions, site accommodation, safety equipment, and the overhead of managing the workforce — the true all-in cost to employ one unskilled construction worker on an organised site is approximately three and a half to four lakh rupees per year. Fifty labourers over a two-year construction timeline: three and a half to four crore rupees just for unskilled labour.

A concrete batching plant costs twenty to thirty lakh rupees. It replaces ten men mixing cement by hand. Operating cost per year: two lakh rupees for maintenance and a single operator. Over ten years, total cost is forty lakh rupees. The labour cost for ten men over ten years: thirty-five to forty lakh rupees. The batching plant pays for itself in Year One.

A robotic rebar tying system costs sixty to eighty lakh rupees. It replaces five to six rebar workers. Over ten years, the labour cost for six workers is two crore ten lakh rupees. The robot — eighty lakh plus twenty lakh in maintenance — totals one crore. Saving: one crore ten lakh rupees.

This is the actual math that actual builders are doing right now. And what the math reveals: for repetitive tasks — cement mixing, rebar tying, bricklaying — the crossover point where robots become cheaper than humans is not in the future. It is now, for organised construction firms with access to capital.

3D Printing.

Apis Cor constructed a fully functional home in less than twenty-four hours using 3D concrete printing. The printer extrudes concrete layer by layer, following a digital design. It builds walls, doorways, window frames — the entire structure — in a single continuous process. No bricks to lay. No mortar to mix. No scaffolding to climb. A 3D-printed house requires five technicians. A conventionally built house of the same size requires thirty to forty labourers working for six weeks.

The precision of 3D printing means nearly zero material waste. A conventional building site wastes fifteen to twenty percent of cement and bricks. A 3D printer uses exactly the amount of concrete in the design file. No more. 3D printers are now being used for multi-story buildings, bridge sections, and infrastructure components. The technology is scaling.

Prefabrication.

The technology that will displace the most workers is not robots on-site. It is the elimination of the site itself.

In China, Broad Sustainable Building constructed a thirty-story building in fifteen days using prefabricated modules. Not fifteen months. Fifteen days. The modules were built in a factory over three months, then trucked to the site and assembled. Broad Group demonstrated five-day assembly of a twenty-six-story tower by prefabricating complete twelve-metre volumetric units with mechanical, electrical, and plumbing pre-installed in the factory.

A building constructed on-site the traditional way employs one hundred workers for twelve months. The same building, prefabricated in a factory and assembled on-site, employs thirty workers at the factory and ten workers on-site for assembly. The factory jobs require training. The assembly jobs require skills Ramesh does not have. The ninety jobs that disappear — carrying bricks, mixing cement, tying rebar — are gone. And the worker never even appears in a "jobs lost" statistic, because he was never hired in the first place.

• • •

THE CHINA LESSON

The construction speed described above is not theoretical. It is operational reality in China, right now, at scale.

China's prefabricated construction market is growing from CNY 1.48 trillion in 2024 to CNY 2.47 trillion by 2029. Chinese construction companies are now exporting their technology. When a Chinese company bids for a metro project in Delhi or a highway project in Maharashtra, they bring their methods — prefabricated bridge sections, automated tunnel boring, modular station components. And when they win contracts — as they are winning contracts across Asia and Africa — the Indian construction labour model encounters technology it has never seen.

More than the technology, what China demonstrates is the role of government. The Chinese government has committed more than one trillion US dollars to construction, with a significant portion directed toward modular construction. The Ministry of Housing requires thirty percent of new urban floor area to incorporate prefabricated methods by 2027. This is not market evolution. It is policy-driven transformation.

India has announced ambitious infrastructure targets. One hundred smart cities. Housing for all. High-speed rail. Metro networks in fifty cities. What India has not announced is how these will be built. Will they be built using labour-intensive methods that employ seventy million workers today? Or will they be built using the methods that China, Singapore, Japan, and Europe are already deploying — methods that require far fewer workers?

The government has not answered this question. And the silence is its own answer.

• • •

INDIA'S GROWTH DRIVES AUTOMATION — NOT PREVENTS IT

You might be thinking: India's infrastructure needs are enormous. We need one hundred smart cities. We need housing for all. Surely that means more construction jobs, not fewer.

You are half right. India will grow. India's construction boom is real. The demand is genuine. And that is precisely why automation will accelerate.

Three forces are in tension. Demand is increasing — India needs to build more, faster. Speed must increase — the developer who completes a building in six months captures buyers before the developer who takes eighteen months. Cost must decrease — as supply tries to meet demand, cost efficiency determines who survives.

Faster delivery. Lower cost. Higher output. There is only one way to achieve all three simultaneously: automation.

You cannot make construction faster by hiring more workers. Ramesh mixing cement by hand does not mix faster when you give him a second shovel. You make construction faster by replacing Ramesh with a batching plant that mixes continuously. You cannot make construction cheaper by paying workers less — Ramesh is already earning the minimum. You make construction cheaper by replacing one hundred workers with thirty technicians operating robots.

India's growth does not protect construction workers. India's growth is the reason they will be displaced. The very forces driving India's infrastructure boom — demand, speed, cost pressure — are the forces driving automation. The government celebrates both. The Ministry of Housing celebrates smart cities and rapid construction. The Ministry of Skill Development celebrates productivity improvements. Both are correct in their domains. But no ministry tracks Ramesh, who is being automated out of existence by the same growth the nation is celebrating.

• • •

STOP AND COUNT

Stop reading for a moment and count.

How many workers have been described in this book so far who are standing on the edge of displacement?

Security and surveillance: nine to twelve million workers. Agriculture: one hundred and forty-four million landless agricultural labourers. Garments: twenty to twenty-seven million workers over the next decade. Logistics and gig work: twelve million today, twenty-three and a half million projected by 2030. Construction: seventy million workers today.

Add these numbers. You are looking at two hundred and fifty to three hundred million people — a quarter of India's population — whose livelihoods are at risk within the next decade.

And I have not yet covered the back office workers. The data entry clerks. The accountants. The call centre employees. The bank tellers. The retail workers.

If you are not counting, you are not understanding the scale of what is approaching.

• • •

YOU ARE NOT SAFE

If you believe you are safe from this disruption, you are wrong. And your belief that you are safe makes you part of the problem.

You might be a software engineer. You think: I write code. AI cannot replace me. You are partially right. But AI is already writing code. You will not be replaced tomorrow. But the junior developer who would have been hired to assist you will not be hired at all. And in five years, when AI writes eighty percent of routine code, how many software engineers does the industry need? Half as many? A third?

You might be a manager. You think: I make decisions. Robots cannot manage people. You are partially right. But AI is already doing workforce scheduling, performance analytics, and resource allocation. Your job might survive. But your team shrinks from fifteen people to five. What happens to the ten people who used to work for you?

You might be a doctor. You think: medicine requires human judgment. You are partially right. But AI diagnostic systems are already more accurate than human radiologists for certain conditions. The medical laboratory technician? Automated. The medical transcriptionist? Replaced by voice-to-text AI. The hospital administration staff? Reduced by digital systems. You remain. Your support ecosystem shrinks.

You might survive. But the ecosystem you depend on will not.

And here is where your life intersects with Ramesh's. Ramesh builds the apartment you live in. When Ramesh is unemployed, he stops sending eight thousand rupees home to his village. His family stops buying things. The shopkeeper in his village sells less. The shopkeeper orders less from the distributor. The distributor orders less from the factory. The factory produces less. The factory worker earns less.

Ramesh's nephew, who went back to the village when he could not find construction work, is now desperate. He joins two million other desperate young men looking for any income. They apply for the same security guard jobs. The competition drives wages down. Your maid, your driver, your office peon — their wages are suppressed because the labour supply has increased.

And when two hundred and fifty million people across multiple sectors are displaced over a decade, what do you think happens to your city? To law and order? To social stability?

We are one country. We are one community. Our lives are intertwined. When a quarter of the population loses their livelihood within a decade, there is no gated community tall enough to protect you from the consequences.

• • •

THREE WAVES

Construction automation is not one event. It is three waves arriving at different speeds.

Wave One: Factory Automation for Components — Happening Now.

The first wave is already here. Automated batching plants, robotic systems for reinforcement placement, shutter cleaning, concrete finishing — all reducing dependency on manual labour in precast factories and component manufacturing units across India. Workers displaced from factories look for other work. Most move to on-site construction, where they join Ramesh carrying bricks and mixing cement. This wave displaces ten to twelve million workers over the next five years. They do not disappear. They move one step down the skill ladder.

Wave Two: On-Site Robotics — Three to Seven Years.

The second wave is when robots arrive on the building site itself. Bricklaying robots. Rebar tying robots. Autonomous excavators. This is the wave that directly threatens Ramesh. India's construction robotics market reached 5.60 billion dollars in 2024, expected to reach 17.24 billion dollars by 2033 — a growth rate of 13.30

percent. A market tripling in size over nine years means robots are spreading across construction sites at an accelerating pace. When robot costs fall below three million rupees for a complete system, and when rental models make them accessible to mid-sized contractors, Wave Two hits full force. We are three to five years from that point in India's Tier 1 cities. Seven to ten years in Tier 2 and Tier 3. This wave displaces another fifteen to twenty million workers — the Rameshes, the brick carriers, the cement mixers. They will not move to another job in construction. There is no other job. They will move to the informal sector or return to villages where there is also no work.

Wave Three: Full Prefabrication — Seven to Fifteen Years.

The third wave is when construction sites largely disappear and buildings are manufactured in factories and assembled on-site. When India builds its hundred smart cities, its metro networks, its high-speed rail corridors — will it use the same prefabrication methods that China, Japan, and Singapore have already proven? The answer will be yes, because cost and speed will demand it. A building that would have employed one hundred workers on-site for twelve months will instead employ twenty workers in a factory for six months and ten workers on-site for two weeks. The workers who remain will be factory technicians, crane operators, welding specialists, quality inspectors — roles that require training Ramesh does not have and cannot get in three months at an ITI. The government's projection of one hundred million construction workers by 2030 assumes Wave Three does not happen. But Wave Three is not a question of if. It is a question of when. And the gap between the government's projection and reality is where thirty to forty million people will fall through.

• • •

THE SAFETY ARGUMENT

There is an argument for construction automation that is morally unassailable, and it will accelerate adoption faster than economics alone.

Construction is India's most dangerous sector. Falls from scaffolding. Crushing injuries from falling materials. Electrocution. Heat stroke in summer when temperatures on an open building site reach forty-eight degrees. Ramesh has seen three men fall in twelve years. Two survived with broken legs and will never work construction again. One did not survive.

Construction workers face four times the risk of fatal injury compared to workers in other industries. The "Fatal Four" causes — falls, struck-by injuries, electrocutions, and caught-in or between accidents — account for nearly sixty percent of construction fatalities.

Robots do not fall. Robots do not get heat stroke. Robots do not die when a concrete slab collapses. The safety argument for automation is real, powerful, and ethically compelling. And it makes Ramesh's displacement not just economically inevitable but morally defensible.

Here is the tension: I do not want Ramesh to die on a construction site. If a robot can do his work and keep him safe, that is a genuine good.

But what is our responsibility to Ramesh when the robot that saves his life also takes his livelihood? Is his safety improved if he is alive but unemployed, with no alternative income, no skills the market values, and a family that depends on the eight thousand rupees he sends home every month?

The safety argument will be used to accelerate automation without addressing what happens to the displaced workers. "We are making construction safer," the industry will say. And they will be telling the truth. But they will be telling only half the truth. The full truth is: we are making construction safer by removing the workers. And we have no plan for where those workers go next.

If we are going to automate construction for safety reasons — and we should — then we must simultaneously build the transition pathways for the workers we are protecting out of existence. Right now, we are doing the first without the second. And that is not protection. That is abandonment with a safety certificate.

• • •

THE TRAP HAS CLOSED

Twelve years ago, Ramesh walked from one side of a closing trap to the other. He thought he was escaping. He was relocating.

The farm has now automated behind him. Rice transplanting machines do the work of ten labourers. The village that once employed fifty farm labourers now employs ten. He cannot go back – there is nothing to go back to.

The construction site is automating in front of him. The same forces – economics, speed, safety – documented in this chapter are converging on every site where Ramesh mixes cement and ties wire. The city that once employed one hundred construction workers per building now employs thirty. Within a decade it will employ fifteen.

Both sides have closed. The space Ramesh occupied – the space between the automated farm and the automated city – no longer exists.

And the most painful part is this: no ministry tracks the single human being falling through the gap. The Ministry of Agriculture celebrates mechanisation as productivity improvement. The Ministry of Housing celebrates smart cities and rapid construction. Both are correct in their domains. But no ministry measures what happens to the man automated out of existence by both simultaneously.

This is not a coordination failure. It is structural blindness. The way our economy is measured, the way our policies are designed, the way our success is defined – none of it tracks the worker who falls through the gap between sectors. When Ramesh loses his construction job and cannot return to farm work, he does not appear in unemployment statistics if he becomes a street vendor or a daily wage labourer in the informal sector. He is not counted as "displaced by automation." He is just poor. And his poverty is invisible because it is one story among millions.

Multiply Ramesh by seventy million, and you are not talking about individual tragedies. You are talking about a civilisational restructuring of where people live, what they do, and whether the economy has any use for their labour. India has managed massive transitions before – the Green Revolution, Liberalisation, the IT boom. But those transitions created more jobs than they destroyed. This one may not. And the window for planning is measured in years, not decades.

• • •

WHAT COULD BE BUILT

The warning does not end here. If you are reading this book carefully, you are also the kind of person who builds things. Three clear opportunities exist.

One: The Micro-Skilling Platform.

Ramesh cannot go to a six-month ITI course to learn to operate a 3D printer. He cannot afford to stop working for six months. His family eats from what he earns this week. But Ramesh has a smartphone. He uses WhatsApp. He watches videos. Fifteen minutes per day. One skill per month. Delivered in Hindi, Tamil, Telugu, Marathi — the languages construction workers actually speak. No classroom. No certificate exam. Just practical, hands-on video training teaching how to operate a concrete batching plant, how to read a digital blueprint, how to assist a drone operator, how to perform quality inspection using a tablet and an AI-powered app. At the end of three months, Ramesh has skills that make him employable in the construction sites of 2028. He gets a verified digital credential. He commands a higher wage because he has moved from unskilled labour to semi-skilled technician. The factories building prefab modules need trained workers. They are hiring today. But they cannot find workers with the right skills because the training does not exist in a form displaced construction workers can access. The entrepreneur who builds this platform is solving a genuine market problem. This is a business. And it is needed now.

Two: The Construction Worker Cooperative.

Ramesh owns nothing. He owns his labour, and when his labour is no longer needed, he has nothing. But what if ten construction workers pooled their savings and bought one concrete batching plant? Or one small excavator? They form a cooperative. They own the equipment collectively. They rent themselves and the equipment as a package to contractors. The contractor no longer needs to employ ten men mixing cement by hand — he hires the cooperative with the batching plant. The ten men operate the equipment, maintain it, and share the rental income. This model exists in agriculture — small farmers form cooperatives to buy tractors and combine harvesters that no individual can afford. An entrepreneur who specialises in forming these cooperatives — providing the legal structure, arranging the financing, training the members, connecting them to contractors — creates value for everyone.

Three: The Digital Identity and Safety Record.

Ramesh has worked on five different building sites over twelve years. He has no written record of this. No employment letters. No skill certificates. No safety training records. When he goes to a new site, the contractor treats him as unskilled labour. He gets the lowest wage. A digital platform where every construction worker has an identity — every site they work on logs their attendance, their tasks, their safety training, their skills, every contractor rates their reliability — gives Ramesh something transformative when he goes to a new site. He shows his digital profile: "Ramesh has worked 2,847 days on construction sites. He has completed safety training. He has operated a concrete batching plant. His reliability rating is 4.6 out of 5. Zero safety violations." He is no longer unskilled labour. He is a verified, trained, reliable construction worker with a track record. He commands a higher wage. The platform also provides portable accident insurance that follows him from site to site. This is a business. The entrepreneur who builds it is solving a real market inefficiency.

• • •

RAMESH AT FORTY-THREE, HIS SON AT SIXTEEN

Ramesh is forty-three. He has worked construction for twelve years. He has sent eight thousand rupees home every month. His son is sixteen, in eleventh standard, the first in the family to reach this level of education.

In two years, Ramesh's son will finish school. He will look for work. He will not find construction work because the construction work is automated. He will not find farm work because the farm work is automated. He will not find security work because the security work is automated. He will not find delivery work because the delivery work is automated.

He will join the informal economy. He will struggle. He will earn less than his father did. He will look at his father and ask: you worked so hard. You sent me to school. Why does nothing get better?

And Ramesh will not have an answer. Because Ramesh did everything right. He worked hard. He sacrificed. He believed in the promise that effort leads to progress.

That promise is breaking. And it is breaking because of forces Ramesh cannot see, cannot understand, and cannot fight alone.

But you can see these forces. You are reading about them right now. What will you do with what you know?

The water is here. The robots are operational. The prefabrication factories are being built. The AI-powered design systems are generating buildings in minutes. Seventy million workers. Two hundred and fifty million across the sectors covered so far. One quarter of India's population standing on the edge of economic displacement within a decade. The wave is here. The question is not whether it will hit. The question is whether we will manage it together, or whether we will let it break us.

• • •

But I am not done yet. Because there is one sector where millions of people work every day, sitting at computers, believing their work is essential, believing they are educated enough to be safe, believing automation will never reach them.

Come with me to the back office.

• • •

CHAPTER 6: THE BRIDGE HAS BEEN BROKEN

CHAPTER 6

THE BRIDGE HAS BEEN BROKEN

BPO & CALL CENTRES: HOW INDIA LOST ITS FIRST LADDER

THE FIRST JOB THAT CHANGED EVERYTHING

Let me tell you about a certain pride that this country invented.

It was the pride of a young man from Lucknow — a middle-income family, one government-servant father, one mother who had sacrificed her own ambitions quietly — who walked into an air-conditioned office, put on a headset, and for the very first time in his life spoke to someone sitting in London.

Not as a servant.

Not as someone asking for a favour.

As a professional.

As someone being paid to help.

That pride was real.

I heard it in phone calls home —

"Amma, I got the job. The one with the night shift. The salary is twenty-two thousand."

You could hear the family stop breathing on the other end.

This was not just a job. It was the first rung of a ladder India had never offered these families before.

White-collar work.

A fixed salary.

An ID card with an international company's name.

That was the BPO.

And for thirty years, it was real, it was good, and it changed lives.

I have to tell you what is being done to that ladder.

• • •

WHAT IS A BPO? (EXPLAINED SIMPLY, FOR YOU)

Before I tell you what is being destroyed, let me explain what it is.

This chapter is not for industry insiders. It is for you.

BPO stands for Business Process Outsourcing.

That is a complicated phrase for something simple:

A company in America or Britain decides that instead of hiring people in their own country to handle certain jobs — answering customer calls, checking insurance claims, managing payroll, providing technical support — they will send those jobs to India.

India will do them at a fraction of the cost, at the same quality or better.

The jobs that came here were the backbone of every large Western company.

When you call your bank's helpline, someone reads your account details off a screen and follows a script to help you.

When an insurance company in London receives ten thousand claim forms, someone has to check each one.

When a telecom company in Australia has fifty thousand customer bills needing review, someone does the reviewing.

For thirty years, that someone was a young Indian sitting in an office in Bengaluru, Hyderabad, Pune, or Gurgaon.

KPO — Knowledge Process Outsourcing — is the elder sibling.

If BPO is about following a process, KPO is about applying judgment:

Legal research.

Financial analysis.

Medical data.

Patent filing.

KPO workers needed higher qualifications and were paid more.

Many BPO workers who stayed and kept learning made that climb.

That journey — from answering calls to analysing balance sheets — was the industry's most beautiful story.

Exposure to the world through a headset could genuinely change a life.

India built an empire on this.

By 2024, India was handling 52% of the world's business process outsourcing.

Not 10%.

More than half.

1.65 million people worked in BPO and call centre roles.

Another 3.5 million in the wider IT and business services ecosystem.

These were salaried, PF-deducted, health-insured professionals.

India's first generation of white-collar workers who needed neither a government job nor a family connection.

They needed English, a graduation certificate, and the will to show up.

That era is ending.

And the people who will be hurt first are not sitting in Bengaluru's glass towers.

They are in Indore.

In Jaipur.

In Nagpur.

In your city, reading this.

• • •

THE MACHINE THAT NEVER SLEEPS, NEVER ARGUES, NEVER TAKES A DIWALI BREAK

To understand what is coming, understand what a BPO worker actually does all day.

They repeat.

They follow a script.

They listen to a problem, match it to a known solution, and deliver it.

The call about a wrong credit card charge has a script.

A call about the cancelled flight has a script too.

The document to be checked for the correct date of birth and right policy number has a process — so defined, so rule-based, that it can be written step by step.

And anything that can be written down step by step can be taught to a machine.

The AI systems arriving in India's BPOs are software programmes that listen to a caller's voice, understand meaning and intent — not just keywords — and respond in a warm, patient human voice.

They do not need a toilet break every two hours.

They do not get short with an angry caller at the end of a twelve-hour shift.

They do not request Diwali off.

The moment one call ends, they answer the next.

Think of what that means in plain money.

One AI system costs approximately one lakh rupees a month.

One AI system replaces fifteen human agents.

That works out to six thousand six hundred rupees per "agent" — less than what a BPO worker in the cheapest Tier-3 city takes home.

No Indian worker — no matter how low the cost of living in their town — can compete with that arithmetic.

But the cost is not even the most important part.

Here is what should keep you up at night:

Every call the AI system handles makes it smarter — and that learning is instantly shared across every connected machine in the network.

When ten million calls have been processed, every bot in the system knows what ten million calls taught it.

A human agent who handles sixty calls a day for an entire career handles perhaps a million calls in a lifetime.

The AI handles ten million in a few months.

And it never forgets a single one.

This is not the machine being better at the job.

This is the machine rewriting what expertise means.

THE WAVE HAS ALREADY HIT. YOU JUST HAVEN'T FELT IT YET.

I want to show you a number that should stop you cold.

In the year 2021 to 2022, India's BPO sector added 177,000 new jobs.

The industry was a heartbeat — strong, regular, reliable.

The year after: 130,000 jobs.

Still beating, though slower.

Then came 2023 to 2024: fewer than 17,000 jobs.

And the year after: fewer than 17,000 again.

From 177,000 to 17,000 in two years.

The industry's revenue kept growing.

The big companies' profits kept growing.

The heartbeat did not stop — it went into arrhythmia.

That gap between growing revenue and frozen headcount is not a mystery.

That gap is where the AI went.

And then there is Megha.

Megha S. was thirty-two years old.

She had been working at a Bengaluru software firm for years, earning eight lakh rupees annually — a settled life, a career she had built carefully.

She was laid off in October 2025, just before the festive season.

Dussehra was ending.

Diwali was three weeks away.

Her manager sat across from her and said:

You are the first one who has been replaced by AI.

> *"I was told I am the first one who has been replaced by AI." — Megha S., Bengaluru, October 2025*

She did not tell her parents.

Imagine that Diwali.

She goes home.

Her mother has made the sweets she loves.

The diyas are lit.

The house smells of ghee and marigolds.

Her father asks how work is.

She smiles.

Fine, she says.

She picks up a ladoo and puts it in her mouth.

And it tastes like nothing.

Because the thing she cannot say is sitting in her chest like a stone.

She avoids her mother's eyes when the question comes again:

"Are they treating you well? Is there a promotion coming?"

She nods.

She looks at the diya.

The flame blurs.

This is not a statistic.

This is a person.

She will not be the last.

• • •

THE MEN WHO BUILT TOMORROW ARE TELLING YOU WHAT HAPPENS TO TODAY

On February 16th, 2026, at India's own AI Summit in New Delhi, the man who co-founded Sun Microsystems — whose technology became the backbone of the internet, who gave India its IT boom — stood at the podium and said this:

> *"By 2030, there will be no such thing as IT services. There will be no such thing as BPO. Those are gone."*

Gone.

Not "shrinking."

Not "transforming."

Gone.

Vinod Khosla was not done:

> *"IT and BPO services will disappear, almost certainly within the next five years. The 250 million young people in India should be selling AI-based products and services to the rest of the world. Almost no economist or business manager is thinking about it. It's a huge danger, and we cannot ignore it." — Vinod Khosla*

Read that last line again.

The man who built the technology that gave India its IT and BPO empire says almost no one in a position to do something is thinking about the danger.

He did not say: India has a plan.

He did not say: someone is preparing those 250 million young people.

He said: almost no one is thinking about it.

And then, three days later, on February 19th, someone else spoke at that same summit.

Someone whose voice carries a different kind of weight.

Not the weight of a man who built yesterday's technology —
but the man who is building tomorrow's.

Sam Altman, CEO of OpenAI, stood in New Delhi and said:

> *"India, the world's largest democracy, is well-positioned to lead in AI — not just to build it, but to shape it and decide what our future is going to look like. On our current trajectory, we believe we may be only a couple of years away from early versions of true superintelligence. If we are right, by the end of 2028, more of the world's intellectual capacity could reside inside of data centres than outside of them."*

Let those words settle.

By the end of 2028 — less than three years from today — the total computing intelligence inside the world's data centres could exceed the total intellectual capacity of all 8 billion human beings combined.

Altman acknowledged, without flinching, what this means for work:

> *"The other side of this coin is that current jobs are going to get disrupted as AI can do more and more of the things that drive our economy today. It will be very hard to outwork a GPU in many ways."*

Two men at the same summit, in India, speaking to India.

One says BPO is gone by 2030.

The other says by 2028, AI's collective intelligence will surpass humanity's.

And the building that will employ Solapur's graduates for thirty years is still on a drawing board.

• • •

WHEN THE BANKERS AND THE BUILDER BOTH AGREE

Jefferies, one of the world's largest investment banks, published its assessment in September 2025:

India's call centres will take a 50% revenue hit from AI over the next five years.

Back-office functions — document processing, data entry, quality checks — will take a 35% hit.

India runs 52% of the world's outsourcing.

A 50% revenue cut to a 52% market share is not a corporate inconvenience.

It is a generational employment catastrophe.

And then there is Pramod Bhasin.

Bhasin is the man who built India's first call centre — eighteen employees in Gurgaon in the 1990s, cubicles partitioned by saris strung from the ceiling, handling calls for GE Capital.

He built what became Genpact.

He is, in the truest sense, the man who built the ladder.

"The biggest impact is going to be on young students coming out of college."

— Pramod Bhasin, Reuters, October 2025

The man who built the ladder is watching it being pulled from the wall.

Not quietly.

Loudly.

On the record.

In a Reuters investigation read in fifteen countries.

WHERE DID THEY GO? THE FALL NOBODY IS COUNTING

Here is a question that the industry's annual reports do not answer.

When a BPO sheds ten thousand jobs, where do those people go?

Some found jobs at other BPOs — for now.

The industry still employs 1.65 million people.

Those already inside are holding on.

Those trying to get in cannot.

Some climbed.

The ambitious ones — who had been watching the technology around them, using their BPO exposure to learn, to observe, to understand — pivoted.

Analytics.

Digital marketing.

IT coordination.

Customer experience consulting.

These are real success stories.

They exist.

They are a minority.

The majority went somewhere India's economy is very efficient at absorbing people with nowhere else to go:

The gig economy.

India's gig workforce grew from 7.7 million in 2020–21 to over 12 million by 2024–25.

It will reach 23.5 million by 2030.

That growth is read as flexibility and opportunity.

But behind every Swiggy rider who speaks excellent English, who knows how to operate a computer, who uses the word "SLA" correctly in casual conversation — there is sometimes a former BPO agent.

The headset is gone.

The air-conditioned office is gone.

The ID card is gone.

What remains is a two-wheeler, a phone, a forty-degree afternoon, and twenty-two thousand rupees a month after fuel.

No PF.

No ESI.

No sick leave.

No promotion cycle.

The white-collar worker became a gig worker.

The broken scaffolding became the street.

Nobody counts this.

The government does not publish a table called "Former BPO Workers Now Delivering Food."

But ask anyone managing a large urban delivery fleet whether they have educated, English-speaking riders who clearly came from something better.

The answer is yes.

And this is the insight that changes everything.

These people are not unskilled.

They are mis-deployed.

They know computers.

They understand customer journeys and business processes.

They have worked with international clients.

They know what a CRM is, what a ticket is, what a quality score is.

They are disciplined, tech-comfortable, process-trained.

Add ninety days of focused AI skill-building, and you have not retrained a displaced worker.

You have created something India has never had before — and desperately needs.

• • •

THE WAVE IS COMING TO YOUR CITY. NOT BENGALURU'S. YOURS.

You have read about layoffs at big Bengaluru BPOs.

You may have thought:

That is the big city.

Those are the glass offices.

We are different here.

Let me tell you about Indore.

Indore has 30,000 BPO seats.

Teleperformance — the world's largest customer experience company — operates there.

The city attracted these companies precisely because it was not Bengaluru:

Lower rent.

Younger workers.

Average age twenty-four.

Loyal staff who would not leave for two thousand rupees more per month elsewhere.

Those same qualities now make Indore doubly exposed.

The AI system that costs one lakh a month costs the same in Indore as in Bengaluru.

Automation mathematics does not care about your city's cost of living.

But the workers in Indore have fewer exits.

There is no Infosys campus nearby to absorb them.

There is the BPO.

And then there is what was there before the BPO.

Jaipur: 25,000 seats.

Coimbatore: 30,000.

Chandigarh: 20,000.

Lucknow, Bhubaneswar, Nagpur, Raipur.

All built BPO operations on government land and with government support through the India BPO Promotion Scheme under Digital India.

The government spent real money to bring white-collar jobs to smaller cities.

And now those same government-funded centres are the most exposed.

They were designed for the old model:

Scale.

Repetition.

Low cost.

The old model is being automated.

If you are in Indore today and your BPO is still hiring, I am not asking you to panic.

I am asking you to look at what happened in Bengaluru two years ago.

What happened there is the signal.

Your city is next.

The only question is whether you use the time you have left.

THE SCAFFOLDING CAN BE BUILT HIGHER. BUT ONLY IF WE START NOW.

I have told you what is falling.

Now let me tell you what could be built instead.

And why the people who lost the most are the ones best placed to lead the rebuilding.

• • •

THE AI OFFICER: INDIA'S MOST URGENT NEW PROFESSION

India has over 63 million small and medium enterprises.

Every shop.

Factory.

Transport company.

Medical clinic.

School.

Most are watching the AI revolution through news articles and thinking:

This is for large companies.

This is not for me.

They are wrong.

AI tools today are so accessible that a company with ten employees can automate:

Customer follow-ups.

Invoice checks.

Social media.

HR paperwork.

Sales calls.

The technology exists.

What is missing is the person who knows how to set it up and keep it running.

That person has a name.

The AI Officer.

Every company in India needs one.

Not a software engineer earning fifteen lakhs a year.

A practical, operational person who understands AI tools, can identify which one solves which problem, can set them up without a computer science degree, and can train colleagues to use them.

The former BPO worker already knows:

How to use computers and CRM systems.

How customer journeys work.

How to manage a workflow.

How to meet a quality target.

How to work with international standards.

These are not small skills.

These are exactly the foundations on which AI deployment skills sit.

Add ninety days of focused, practical training — how to use AI for customer service automation, document processing, data analysis, workflow management, content creation — and that person can walk into any SME in their district and immediately add value.

The economics work for everyone.

A trained AI Officer earns thirty-five to fifty thousand rupees a month — significantly better than BPO floor wages.

The SME that hires them saves lakhs per year by automating processes they currently do manually.

The displaced worker gets a better position than the one they lost.

Nobody is charity.

Everybody earns.

Sixty-three million SMEs.

One AI Officer each.

That is not a programme.

That is a transformation of the Indian economy.

• • •

SKILL AI: THE POLICY CHANGE THAT CHANGES EVERYTHING

The Skill India Mission has trained millions in welding, electrical work, construction, and hospitality.

These are good skills.

They are also the skills of the economy we had.

The recommendation of this book is this:

Skill India must become Skill AI.

Not as a rebrand.

As a genuine reorientation.

Six-month courses available in every district, in local languages, subsidised by the government and co-funded by private sector companies who will hire the graduates.

Not theory.

Not programming.

Not mathematics.

Practical AI tools.

At the end of six months, the graduate can add value to any Indian company from day one.

The investment is a fraction of what India spends on job creation schemes that no longer match reality.

The return is a generation of young Indians who are not racing against AI — because they are the people who make AI useful for others.

India supplied the world's back-office workforce for thirty years.

It can now supply the world's AI deployment workforce.

The practitioners who take AI built in Silicon Valley and make it work for a kirana store in Kanpur, a clinic in Coimbatore, a transport company in Nashik, a factory in Faridabad.

That is a market of hundreds of millions of businesses globally.

And India — with its English fluency, its technology exposure, its young population, and its BPO heritage — is positioned to own it.

• • •

A LETTER TO SOLAPUR: THE CITY THAT DESERVES A BETTER PLAN

I need to speak now not as a writer, but as a son.

Solapur is my paternal hometown.

On August 18th, 2025, Chief Minister Devendra Fadnavis announced that Solapur will receive Maharashtra's second-largest IT park.

Fifty acres on Hotgi Road.

Investment: approximately thirty-eight crore rupees.

Target: 45,000 jobs.

Timeline: eighteen months.

The instinct is right.

But here is the question:

By the time this IT park opens, what kind of world will it open into?

The IT park opens in late 2027.

Superintelligence — by projection — in 2028.

Vinod Khosla says IT services and BPO will be gone by 2030.

A park built for traditional IT services would open one year before the world that needs traditional IT services ceases to exist.

Building the wrong thing in the right place is still the wrong thing.

So build something else.

An AI Park.

An AI Training Campus.

An AI Solutions Hub for SMEs.

An AI Services Centre — the new BPO.

Vernacular AI Research.

AI Infrastructure Backbone.

Solapur becomes not just a city that uses AI.

But a city that builds AI solutions for the rest of India.

That is a better dream than an IT park.

And it is a dream Solapur is ready to dream.

• • •

THE SCAFFOLDING GETS TALLER – BUT SOMEONE HAS TO BUILD IT

I began with pride.

The pride of a headset and a phone call to London and a call home to Amma.

That pride was real.

The jobs were real.

The lives built on those salaries were real.

But the headset is being replaced.

Not someday.

Now.

In Bengaluru, the wave has already hit.

In Indore and Jaipur, you can see it building offshore.

And Solapur is planning a resort on the beach — while the tsunami is already in the water.

The question is not dramatic.

It is practical.

It is urgent.

Are we training India's young people for the world that is here — Or the world that is gone?

The former BPO worker delivering food on a Swiggy bike in July rain, speaking perfect English, knowing exactly what an SLA is —

That person is not finished.

They are the people India needs.

The AI Officer every SME is waiting for.

They are the future —

If someone builds the bridge to get them there.

The bridge was broken.

Build a better one.

By now, a question should be forming in your mind.

We have travelled through five sectors — security guards, farmers, garment workers, logistics drivers, and now the people at the call centre.

Each chapter has shown a different industry.

Different workers.

Different cities.

Different timelines.

But the thing doing the disrupting is always the same.

The same AI system that learned to monitor a building is being taught to drive a truck.

The same pattern-recognition technology that automated a garment inspection line is now handling a customer complaint.

The same machine.

Different rooms.

That is what the next chapter is about:

Not what is being lost —

But who is holding the tool —

And what we do about it.

CHAPTER 7

THE SAME TOOL.

A DIFFERENT PAIR OF HANDS.

THE YELLOW BUILDING

There is a government health centre in a village in rural Maharashtra.

It is a concrete building, painted yellow, with a list of health worker names on a board outside. The board says a doctor is posted here.

A woman arrived at seven in the morning. She has been travelling since before five. Her child has had a cough for three weeks — the kind that does not improve, that wakes the child at night, that the woman has been watching the way mothers watch things they are afraid to name. She brought the child's documents in a cloth bag. She brought food for the day, because she knows how these visits go. The ASHA worker — the health volunteer from her village who told her to come — is with her.

They have been sitting on a bench outside the consultation room since seven.

It is now ten.

The doctor is posted here.

The doctor is not here.

THE GAP BETWEEN THE BOARD AND THE PERSON

This is not unusual.

India has roughly one doctor for every 1,272 people. That number sounds almost manageable until you understand the distribution — most doctors are in cities, most are in specific states, and the gap between the doctors that government health centres are sanctioned to have and the doctors who actually show up is measured in tens of thousands of unfilled posts.

The yellow building exists.

The board exists.

The posted name exists.

The person does not.

Now I need to tell you what arrived in this same building, in this same month, while the woman waits on the bench.

• • •

THE MACHINE THAT CAN READ AN X-RAY

A company called Qure.ai, founded in Mumbai, has built an artificial intelligence system that reads chest X-rays.

Not assists someone in reading them.

Reads them.

The system processes an X-ray image and identifies, in under one second, the probability of tuberculosis, pneumonia, pleural effusion, and fourteen other conditions.

Independent peer-reviewed studies in The Lancet and PLOS Digital Health found that the system matched or outperformed experienced radiologists.

The World Health Organization has updated its tuberculosis screening policy to recommend AI software of this type as a replacement reader — not an assistant — in settings where radiologists are not available.

The government deployed this system as part of India's National TB Elimination Programme.

A PATH TB REACH project in Nagpur put qXR across eight private X-ray laboratories to actively find TB cases in the community. It screened 10,481 presumptive TB patients. No radiologist needed to be physically present for any of them. The AI read each image. The health worker received the result.

The Ministry of Health reports that AI-enabled tools like this contributed to a 27 percent decline in adverse TB outcomes in the national programme.

India has more new tuberculosis cases than any country in the world. India also has, in its rural areas, approximately one radiologist per 100,000 people.

These two facts have coexisted for decades.

The AI does not fix this completely. But it means that a chest X-ray can be read with specialist-level accuracy in the yellow building in the village.

If the X-ray machine is there.

If the system is installed and connected.

The machine is in this building.

The system is connected today.

The woman's child has a chest X-ray. The AI flags a high probability of tuberculosis. A health worker sends the result by phone to a doctor in the district hospital, two hours away. The doctor reviews the flag within the hour. Treatment begins.

The child goes home with medicine instead of with the cough.

THREE MONTHS LATER

Same building.

Same village.

Three months later, the X-ray machine has broken — a part has failed and the replacement has not arrived because the supply chain for government health equipment in this district is what it is.

The connection is also down today. It comes and goes.

A woman arrives with a child who has the same cough. Same cloth bag. Same ASHA worker. Same bench.

The doctor is still posted here. Still not here.

The X-ray machine is broken.

The system is not connected.

The AI cannot read what cannot be taken.

The child goes home with the cough.

THE SAME TOOL. A DIFFERENT PAIR OF HANDS.

That is the whole story of this chapter.

And it is the most important thing in this book.

AI AS DISPLACEMENT – AND AS ACCESS

Every chapter before this one has shown you AI arriving as a displacement — the camera replacing the watchman, the robot approaching the garment line, the drone being tested in place of the delivery boy.

That is true.

AI is doing that.

But AI is also doing something else.

Catching cancer without a hospital.

Teaching a child in Hindi at his exact level.

Translating a Supreme Court judgment into Marathi so a woman knows what her rights are.

Giving a loan to a gig worker who has never been inside a bank.

Warning a farmer that the river will flood in three days.

These are not promises.

They are not pilot projects from a technology conference.

They are things happening.

Measured. Verified. Real.

And the people who are not receiving them — the people who need them most and are last in line for them — are the same people this book has been talking about since the first page.

That is the injustice this chapter is about.

Not that the tool does not work.

That it works — and the wrong pair of hands is holding it.

THE DOCTOR WHO IS NEVER THERE – AND THE ONE WHO ALWAYS IS

India's Primary Health Centre system runs, across most of India, on a permanent staffing deficit.

This is the gap into which AI has arrived.

Not to replace the doctor.

To do what the doctor was never there to do.

TELEMEDICINE AT SCALE

The eSanjeevani platform is the government's telemedicine system.

Since its launch, it has conducted 282 million consultations.

Between April 2023 and November 2025, twelve million of those patients received AI-recommended differential diagnoses – the system suggesting likely conditions based on symptoms, allowing the remote doctor to confirm or refine.

Two hundred and eighty-two million consultations.

From people for whom the journey to a doctor was once a day's travel and a day's wages lost.

CATCHING CANCER WITHOUT A MAMMOGRAM

A startup called Niramai detects breast cancer from thermal scans.

No mammogram.

No radiation.

No refrigerator-sized machine.

The AI reads thermal patterns and flags abnormal heat.

Early detection moves the moment of diagnosis.

That earlier moment is often the difference between life and death.

PREVENTABLE BLINDNESS

India has more than 100 million people with diabetes.

A system called MadhuNetrAI reads retinal images at primary care level. The ophthalmologist reviews only flagged cases.

The reach of expertise extends into villages the specialist will never visit.

THE TUTOR WHO SPEAKS YOUR LANGUAGE

The ASER report measures what children actually know. Millions of children are enrolled in school and learning almost nothing.

A company called Educational Initiatives built an adaptive learning platform called Mindspark.

It teaches at the child's actual level, adjusting every question.

Researchers at J-PAL found that children using Mindspark learned two to three times more than those who did not.

Four hundred thousand children have used it.

India has 250 million enrolled in school.

The gap is not technological.

It is political.

THE LAW WAS ALWAYS IN ENGLISH

The Supreme Court uses SUVAS to translate judgments into vernacular languages.

More than 36,000 Supreme Court decisions translated into Hindi. More than 17,000 into sixteen regional languages.

The Tele-Law programme had reached over one crore beneficiaries by January 2025.

Rights always existed.

Access did not.

THE CREDIT HISTORY YOU NEVER KNEW YOU HAD

One hundred and sixty million Indians have no formal credit history.

AI credit scoring reads UPI patterns and digital traces.

India's UPI infrastructure and Aadhaar reduce the cost of acquiring a bank customer dramatically.

The delivery worker paying his mobile bill every month has unknowingly built a financial profile.

The system can now read it.

But the agricultural labourer paid in cash remains invisible.

The moneylender still has her.

WARNING THE VILLAGE BEFORE THE FLOOD

In Assam's Cachar district, an AI-based emergency management application called RAHAT coordinates flood response.

India Meteorological Department integrates AI into forecasting.

Google Flood Hub provides hyper-local predictions.

The tool works.

The last mile does not always.

THE SAME PATTERN, FIVE TIMES

AI reading a chest X-ray.
AI teaching a child at his level.
AI translating a judgment.
AI giving first-time credit.
AI warning before a flood.
Five domains.
Five working tools.
And in every one of them, access depends on:
Reliable electricity.
Internet connectivity.
A smartphone.
A trained intermediary.
The watchman from Odisha.
The rice-transplanting woman in Bengal.
The garment worker in Tirupur.
The delivery boy from Bihar.
They are at the back of the queue.
The same tool.
Different hands.

WHAT NEEDS TO BE BUILT

1. The AI Intermediary

A trained, paid, AI-literate community professional who bridges the gap between tool and citizen.

2. Offline-First AI

AI systems designed to function fully without reliable internet.

3. Portable Digital Identity

A worker-owned digital profile aggregating financial, work, and health records — readable across systems.

THE CLOSE

Let me go back to the PHC one more time.

The woman has been sitting on the bench for three hours. The ASHA worker beside her is apologetic in the way that people are apologetic when they are complicit in a system and have no power to change it. The child is tired. The cloth bag with the documents is on the woman's lap.

Now imagine a different morning. Same building. Same woman. Same child. But in this version, the district had a health officer who fought for three years to get the digital infrastructure upgraded. Who filled out the forms. Who made the calls. Who knew that qXR could be installed and connected for less than the cost of the equipment that was already supposed to be there and wasn't. Who understood that in this district, in this year, the tool that could save the child's life was available, affordable, and waiting for someone to say yes.

The X-ray is taken. The AI reads it in under a second. The flag goes to the district hospital. The doctor responds within the hour. The child begins treatment.

The ASHA worker does not need to apologise this morning. The woman does not need to wait until noon for someone to tell her to come back tomorrow. Same building. Same child. Different outcome. Not because of a different tool. Because of a different choice.

• • •

The tools are here. The AI that is displacing the watchman is the same family of tools as the AI that is catching cancer in a village health camp. The AI that is replacing the garment worker is the same family of tools as the AI that is teaching a first-generation student in Hindi at his exact learning level. The AI that is training the drone that will replace the delivery boy is the same family of tools as the AI that warns the farmer the river is rising. One tool. Many possible hands.

• • •

The question of whose hands it reaches is not a technology question. It was never a technology question. It is a question about what we value, who we build for, and how urgently we act when we know that the window for building the right way is not unlimited.

That window is measurable in years, not decades. The displacement is already accelerating. The access gap, if we do not close it deliberately and urgently, will become a chasm in the same timeframe.

But — and this is the thing I refuse to let you leave this chapter without holding — the gap is closable. Every example in this chapter is proof. Qure.ai is proof. Mindspark is proof. SUVAS is proof. Tele-Law is proof. The UPI credit model is proof. The tools work. The question is whether we deploy them with the same urgency that the displacement is arriving with.

The uncle in me has been warning you since the prologue about what is coming. But the uncle in me also knows that not every wave destroys. Some waves, caught right, at the right moment, with the right preparation — some waves lift.

The same water. A different response. That is still — just barely — possible.

This chapter held hope. Real hope — earned, evidenced, documented. But if you read carefully, you noticed who it did not fully reach. Every tool described here required at least a foothold in the digital world — a UPI account, a connected health camp, a gram panchayat that was funded and staffed. That foothold is not nothing. For hundreds of millions of people, it is everything they do not have.

The agricultural labourer who earns in cash and has no smartphone. The older worker who lost her garment job and is too old to retrain and too poor to wait. The construction worker's wife in a village that has no electricity after six in the evening. The ones for whom the moneylender is not a problem — he is the only system that has ever seen them at all.

This book has been writing about them since the first page. But it has not yet looked directly at them — at what their lives look like when the displacement arrives and the safety net does not. That is the final reckoning before we close. That is Chapter 8.

CHAPTER 8: THE ONES WE LEFT BEHIND

CHAPTER 8

THE ONES WE LEFT BEHIND

A BRIEF RECKONING BEFORE WE GET TO YOU.

I owe you a confession.

This book set out to be thorough. One chapter per sector, one sector at a time, building the case brick by brick. But India's workforce is vast beyond measure. If I gave every threatened sector its full chapter, this book would be five volumes and you would give up halfway through Volume Two.

So before we move on to the chapter that is directly about you — the educated professional, the office worker, the person who believed they were watching all of this from a safe distance — I need to stop and do something honest. I need to briefly name the workers we did not cover. Because they exist. Their numbers are real. Their vulnerability is as complete as the garment worker's or the delivery boy's. And they deserve to be seen, even if briefly.

Think of this chapter as a corridor. We walk through it quickly. But every door we pass has someone behind it. And every door is going to open.

RETAIL

Her name is Poonam. She has worked at the same neighbourhood clothing store in Malad, Mumbai, for eleven years. She knows every regular customer by name. She remembers that Mrs. Sharma prefers kurtas with elbow-length sleeves and that the college girl who comes every month needs petites. She can tell, from the way a customer touches a fabric, whether they are going to buy or just browse. This knowledge — intimate, accumulated, irreplaceable — is her entire career.

India's retail sector employs somewhere between 40 and 50 million people. It is the second largest employer in the country, after agriculture. Most of these workers are in unorganised retail — the kirana shops, the clothing stores, the hardware shops, the vegetable vendors, the small electronics dealers. They are, in the language of this book, workers with short repetition cycles: serve a customer, make a sale, restock a shelf, repeat.

What is replacing Poonam's knowledge is not a robot that walks the shop floor. It is something quieter and faster. It is an app that already knows what you want before you enter the store. Amazon India and Flipkart now have AI systems that study your purchase history, your browsing behaviour, the time you shop, the price points you click on, and the items you look at but do not buy. They do not need Poonam's eleven years of memory. They have yours.

Quick commerce has arrived at scale. Blinkit, Swiggy Instamart, and Zepto now deliver groceries and everyday goods in ten to thirty minutes, from dark stores that have no shop floor, no customer interaction, and no Poonam. Blinkit alone grew 122 percent year-on-year in FY2024 and added 149 new dark stores. These warehouses are optimised for robotic picking, not human service. The cashier at the organised retail chain faces the same pressure from a different direction: self-checkout kiosks and cashierless store technology are in active deployment by large retailers who are watching their labour costs and doing the arithmetic.

The kirana store may survive. Poonam may not. The neighbourhood shop can adapt — pivot to delivery, to hyper-local convenience, to the things an app cannot do. But that requires a different Poonam: one who can manage an app, track inventory on a phone, coordinate a Swiggy store partnership. The woman who learned to read customers by touch has eleven years of the wrong skill.

The number of retail workers whose jobs are at risk from e-commerce compression, cashierless technology, and AI-driven demand forecasting is not precisely counted in any government survey. That absence itself tells you something about how seriously this country is thinking about the problem.

HEALTHCARE

This is the sector everyone points to when they want to feel safe about automation. 'AI cannot replace a doctor,' they say. And they are broadly right. The doctor who reads your face, holds your wrist, hears what you are not saying — that doctor is not going anywhere for a long time.

But the healthcare system is not just doctors.

Consider the medical transcriptionist. Her job is to listen to a doctor's voice recording and type it into a written medical report. It is painstaking, detail-oriented work. She has been doing it for eight years and she does it accurately. Speech recognition software combined with AI can now do this task at a fraction of the cost, around the clock, without breaks. Globally, medical transcription is already 99 percent automated. In India, the transition is underway. The women who built careers in this work — and it is overwhelmingly women — are watching it disappear.

The lab technician runs routine diagnostic tests: blood counts, urine analyses, slide readings, basic pathology. India has more than one lakh diagnostic labs. Most of them employ technicians who repeat the same tests hundreds of times a day. The repetition cycle is measured in minutes. Automated laboratory equipment combined with AI analysis can process these tests faster and with fewer errors. The Indian laboratory automation market is growing at pace, already valued at more than Rs 2,500 crore and rising sharply. The machine does not replace the entire lab — but it replaces the entry-level technician who was your way into the lab.

A medical billing and coding clerk processes insurance claims. A pharmacy dispenser counts pills and checks prescriptions. The hospital appointment scheduler fills slots in a calendar. These are not glamorous jobs. They are steady, reliable, income-generating jobs that support millions of families. And every single one of them has a repetition cycle short enough to automate.

The sector that everyone said AI could not touch turns out to have millions of workers at the bottom of it who are entirely touchable.

EDUCATION

In every Indian city, and in most towns, and in a surprising number of villages, there is a person who gives tuition. They teach children for two hours in the evening. They charge between Rs 1,000 and Rs 5,000 a month per student. They know their students' weaknesses. They call parents when a child is struggling. They coach not just subjects but confidence. India has an estimated 7.1 crore students enrolled in private tuition. The coaching industry alone is worth more than Rs 58,000 crore a year. Lakhs of people make their living from this parallel education system.

OpenAI's Study Mode, released in 2025, is an AI tutor that explains concepts, answers questions, adapts to a student's level, and works in multiple languages. It does not tire. It does not judge. It does not charge Rs 2,000 a month per subject. A ChatGPT Plus subscription costs roughly Rs 1,700 a month in total — for unlimited tutoring across every subject, at any hour, in the student's own language.

For a family in a smaller city who is currently paying Rs 8,000 a month for tuition across three subjects, the arithmetic is not complicated.

The argument against AI tutors is that they lack human warmth, that they cannot replicate the teacher who notices a child is distracted and adjusts. This is true. For now. It is the same argument that was made about ATMs when they were introduced. Nobody disputes that a human bank teller provides a warmer experience. And yet.

The tuition teacher who can teach students to use AI effectively — who can serve as a guide and a coach rather than just a source of answers — will survive this. The tuition teacher whose entire value is subject knowledge that an AI can now deliver more cheaply is in serious trouble. A coaching centre whose business model is large classrooms, standardised content, and high fees is looking at direct disruption from a platform that is infinitely scalable and costs almost nothing per student.

In formal schools, AI is already automating grading, attendance tracking, and lesson planning. Teachers will not be replaced in bulk — not yet, not soon. But the support staff around teachers, the administrative staff who manage paperwork and schedules, and the massive parallel industry of private tutoring? The wave is already at the door.

DOMESTIC WORKERS

I include them here because no serious account of India's working poor is complete without them. An estimated four to five crore people in India work as domestic helpers, cooks, cleaners, drivers, and caregivers. Most are women. Most are migrants. Almost none have a formal employment contract.

Today they are not primarily threatened by AI — the robotics required to replicate a human cook or a skilled caregiver in an Indian home context is not yet economically viable at scale. Their threat is more indirect: when the delivery boy loses his job, when the garment worker's factory automates, when the family's income compresses, the first expense a household reduces is the maid's salary or the cook's engagement. The automation of other sectors trickles down to the most informal workers through the spending power of the households that employ them.

There are also robotic vacuum cleaners, smart appliances, and AI-managed household systems beginning to replace discrete tasks. The middle-class household that once needed a full-time maid to sweep and mop now has a robot vacuum running on a timer. This is not mass displacement yet. But the direction is set.

I will not spend more time here. The domestic worker deserves a full chapter. She does not have one in this book. That is a failure of space, not of importance.

THE PATTERN, ONE MORE TIME

You have now seen it across seven sectors and four more briefly. Security. Agriculture. Garments. Logistics. Construction. BPO.

And now — passing through quickly but not without acknowledgment — retail, healthcare, education, and domestic work.

The pattern does not change. The technology exists. The economics are moving. The workers are unwarned. The silence is institutional.

And in every sector, the workers most at risk share one thing: their work repeats. Their repetition cycle is short. Seconds, minutes, hours. They sell their time doing the same thing over and over, and AI is a machine that does the same thing over and over, without rest, without complaint, without a salary.

• • •

I want to ask you something. While you were reading these chapters, who were you thinking about? The security guard you pass every morning? A relative who works in a factory? The delivery boy whose face you have never learned? Someone else's problem, in someone else's life?

I have been watching you read. You have been very comfortable so far. You work in an office. You have a degree. You carry a laptop. You use ChatGPT to draft emails and think that makes you AI-literate. You look at everything we have covered and feel sympathy — real, genuine sympathy — for the people being displaced. But not fear. Not for yourself.

That is about to change.

The next chapter is not about someone else. It is about the marketing manager, the accountant, the junior lawyer, the salesperson, the HR executive. It is about the person who spent twelve years building a career in a profession they were told was safe. It is about the work that happens on the fourteenth floor, in the glass office, behind the laptop that always has seventeen tabs open.

It is about you.

There is a specific kind of confidence that a good education produces. It is not arrogance, exactly. It is more like a deep, settled assumption — that the world is ordered in a certain way, that credentials mean something, that the rungs of the ladder are fixed, and that anyone who climbed them properly will not be asked to climb back down. This confidence is not vanity. It is a reasonable conclusion drawn from a lifetime of evidence. It has just been proved wrong.

The professionals who watched the wave take the security guard, the farmer, the garment worker, the delivery boy, the call centre agent — they watched from the shore. They felt safe on high ground. They did not notice that the water was already rising behind them, from the inland side, where no one was looking.

CHAPTER 9: THE PEOPLE WHO THOUGHT

CHAPTER 9

THE PEOPLE WHO THOUGHT

THEY WERE WATCHING FROM THE SHORE

Using a tool is not the same as being irreplaceable.

He works in marketing at a mid-sized company in Gurugram — postgraduate degree, good salary, six years in the role, a team of four people reporting to him. Two phones, always within reach, both with notifications on. Every week, he is in meetings where strategies are debated and campaigns are approved. By any reasonable definition, he is a successful professional.

He also uses ChatGPT. He drafts client emails faster with it, produces first-cut briefs that he then refines, and last month used it to prepare talking points for a presentation. In conversations about AI, he positions himself as someone who has adapted. He is, he believes, ahead of the curve. He is using the technology. He is not afraid of it.

He is not ahead of the curve. He is standing in the water, thinking that wet feet mean he knows how to swim. The wave that is coming does not care about his six years of experience, his postgraduate degree, or the fact that he occasionally uses a chatbot to write emails faster. The wave is specifically designed to do what he does. All of it. Better. Faster. For a fraction of what he costs.

This is the chapter he did not expect to be in.

THE COMFORT THAT IS COSTING YOU

In December 2024, a survey found that 92 percent of Indian knowledge workers were using AI tools in the workplace. India led the world in this measure. Ninety-two percent. We celebrated this. News articles were written. LinkedIn posts were shared. India is an AI-first nation, the headlines declared.

Nobody asked what they were using it for.

The answer: email drafts, meeting summaries, and rephrasing content. These are the top three uses. An intelligent autocomplete for the tasks that were already routine. This is the same as saying that 92 percent of Indian drivers use GPS navigation, and therefore Indian drivers are experts in cartography. They are not. They are better at getting from A to B. They have not become mapmakers.

There is a word for what most Indian professionals are doing with AI right now. It is called augmentation. You use the tool to do your existing job a little faster, a little more easily. This is fine. This is useful. But it is not protection.

Protection comes from being irreplaceable. And using a tool that is designed to replace you is not the same as being irreplaceable. It is, in fact, the opposite. Every time you use ChatGPT to do your job, you are teaching the machine what your job looks like. You are its training data.

The IIM Ahmedabad survey of Indian executives in 2024 found that 60 percent of Indian white-collar workers believe AI will replace jobs in their sector within five years. They are right to believe this. They are wrong about the timeline. It is not five years. Parts of it are already happening. And the most telling number in that survey is not the 60 percent who are worried. It is the number that came with it: only 4 percent of Indian companies have trained more than 50 percent of their staff in AI skills.

Sixty percent worried. Four percent prepared. The gap between those two numbers is the size of the disaster that is coming.

IT ALREADY HAPPENED. YOU JUST DID NOT CALL IT WHAT IT IS.

In the summer of 2025, Tata Consultancy Services announced the reduction of 12,261 jobs. The company was careful about its language. It was not a layoff, they said. It was a 'skill realignment.' The people leaving were not being replaced by machines, they said. The company was simply becoming 'future-ready.'

Here is what was true at the same time: TCS's revenue grew 1.3 percent. Its profits grew 5.9 percent. The company was doing more work than the year before. It did that work with 12,000 fewer people.

More output. Fewer people. That is not a skill realignment. That is a proof of concept.

Infosys, Wipro, and HCL followed similar patterns. Together, India's top IT services firms shed 64,000 employees in FY2024 and another 25,000 to 30,000 in 2025. Campus hiring — the engine that has sent millions of engineering graduates into steady middle-class careers for three decades — fell by more than 60 percent. Infosys, a company that once hired tens of thousands of fresh graduates in a single year, dramatically slowed fresher onboarding. The companies did not say AI was the reason. They said 'market conditions' and 'efficiency.' The machine was polite about it.

But Wipro was less polite in its investor communications. The company deployed more than 200 AI-powered 'intelligent agents' in HR, finance, and legal. Its Chairman said the company is moving toward fully autonomous systems in some areas. Autonomous. Not AI-assisted. Autonomous. The machine operating without a human in the loop.

And PhonePe, one of India's most successful fintech companies, quietly laid off 60 percent of its customer support staff over five years as AI handled more and more of the work. Sixty percent. Not 5 percent. Not 10 percent. Six in ten people whose jobs were to talk to customers, to solve problems, to represent the company — gone.

These are not warnings about the future. They are reports from the present. If you work in IT services, in finance, in any large company — this is the story of your industry, right now, while you are reading this.

WHAT THEY ARE SAYING OUT LOUD

On February 13, 2026 — six days before this book went to print — Mustafa Suleyman, the Chief of Artificial Intelligence at Microsoft, gave an interview to the Financial Times. What he said was not buried in a technical paper. He said it plainly, to a major financial newspaper, knowing it would be published.

He said: "White-collar work, where you're sitting down at a computer, either being a lawyer or an accountant or a project manager or a marketing person — most of those tasks will be fully automated by an AI within the next 12 to 18 months."

The Chief of AI at Microsoft. Not a blogger. Not an alarmist. The man who leads artificial intelligence at the company that makes the software on your office laptop. Twelve to eighteen months.

Dario Amodei, CEO of Anthropic, one of the world's leading AI companies, said something similar: AI could wipe out half of entry-level white-collar jobs. Half.

An LSE professor responded to Suleyman's statement and said white-collar jobs are not going away in 18 months. He is right that full job replacement across the board is not that simple. Jobs are messy. They involve exceptions, judgment calls, human accountability, and coordination that no algorithm yet handles perfectly.

But here is what matters. Even the professor who pushed back said this: "Some single-task, automatable roles will shrink. Many tasks will be automated." He disagrees with the timeline. He does not disagree with the direction.

The wave is coming. The only debate is how fast.

THE DIFFERENCE BETWEEN DOING A JOB AND BEING IRREPLACEABLE

Priya is a marketing manager at a consumer goods company in Mumbai. Eight years of experience. She manages campaigns, writes briefs, presents strategies to leadership, and handles agency relationships. She is good at her job. Priya recently started using AI tools and is genuinely impressed by how much faster she can produce first drafts.

Now look at what Priya actually does in a week. The execution tasks: drafting emails to agency partners, writing campaign briefs, preparing performance reports, building PowerPoint presentations for leadership, proofreading and editing copy. ChatGPT, Jasper AI, and the analytics platform's own auto-reporting tools can do every single one of these. Faster. More consistently. At a fraction of the cost. If you add up the hours Priya spends on execution tasks, they represent most of her working week.

Now, here is what AI cannot do. The judgment tasks: sitting in a room with a difficult client and reading the tension before it becomes a problem. Noticing that the campaign strategy is technically correct but emotionally wrong for the moment the country is living in. Building the trust relationship that makes an agency partner stay late on a Friday to fix a crisis. Taking accountability in a room full of senior leaders when something goes wrong.

Those things — the judgment, the human insight, the accountability, the relationships — are not in Priya's job description. They are the invisible infrastructure that makes her valuable. And the terrible irony is that she has never had to describe those things on a performance review, because they have always been assumed. They were not skills. They were just being a professional.

The professionals who survive will be those who consciously move their work toward the things AI cannot do: judgment in ambiguous situations, accountability for outcomes, client and colleague relationships built on trust, creative insight that connects to the human moment. The ones who will struggle are those who believe that doing a job well is the same as being irreplaceable at it.

This is not a small distinction. It is the distinction that will determine your career.

THE WORK THAT IS BEING AUTOMATED, FUNCTION BY FUNCTION

Here is what is going — not in five years, but now — in the most common white-collar functions.

Marketing and content: 77 percent of marketing professionals already use ChatGPT at work. The AI tools available today — Jasper, Copy.ai, and the large language models — can produce ad copy, blog posts, email campaigns, product descriptions, and social media content at a quality level that would have required a team of three copywriters two years ago. AI is generating landing pages that convert 36 percent better and ads that click through 38 percent better than human-written versions. Entry-level content roles are disappearing. The junior copywriter who once learned the craft by doing is finding there is no entry point left to do it in.

Accounting and finance: 85 percent of routine bookkeeping tasks are automatable, according to US Bureau of Labor projections. AI tools can close the books weekly — not monthly. They can flag anomalies, prepare financial statements, process invoices, run payroll, and generate cash flow forecasts. The entry-level accountant who spent two years doing data entry and reconciliation before being trusted with analysis? That training pipeline is breaking down. The analysis still needs humans. The pipeline into it is disappearing.

Legal support: AI can now review thousands of documents in hours — work that once took teams of junior lawyers weeks. Due diligence that cost Rs 40 lakh now costs Rs 4 lakh. Contract analysis that took two hours per contract takes two minutes. The junior lawyer, the para-legal, the legal researcher — these are the entry-level roles through which people once climbed into senior legal careers. Those roles are being automated first.

Sales and business development: AI Sales Development Representatives can generate leads, write personalised outreach emails, follow up with prospects, qualify them, and schedule meetings. Automatically. Salesforce, Gong, and Conversica already do this. The person who once spent half their workday on prospecting and pipeline management is being asked to do less of it, or finding the job is smaller than it was.

HR: 85 percent of recruitment screening is projected to be automated between 2025 and 2027. The HR associate who filtered resumes and scheduled interviews — one of the most common entry-level professional jobs in Indian companies — is among the most exposed roles in any office.

The pattern is the same everywhere. It begins at the bottom. The entry-level roles are taken first. Then the junior roles. Then the mid-level roles that were being done by people who learned the job by doing the entry-level tasks that no longer exist. The pyramid hollows from the base up.

THE INDIAN PROFESSIONAL: A SPECIFIC VULNERABILITY

India trained an entire generation of professionals for a specific kind of work. Precise, process-driven, execution-oriented. We built the world's largest back office. We became the place where the work gets done — the reports compiled, the code maintained, the accounts processed, the support calls answered.

This was a brilliant strategy for thirty years. It created an enormous middle class. It built Gurugram and Whitefield and Hinjewadi. It sent money home to families in Meerut and Nagpur and Coimbatore. It was the engine of India's service economy.

But it was always execution, not judgment. And execution is precisely what AI does best.

The former HCL Technologies CEO Vineet Nayyar said it plainly: if you believe that Indian IT companies are going to create employment at scale in the coming years, "you must be dreaming." Not a fringe commentator. A man who built one of India's great IT companies.

The Economic Survey of India 2024–25 included, for the first time, a dedicated chapter titled 'Labour in the AI Era: Crisis or Catalyst.' This is the government's own economists asking the question openly. The International Labour Organization's India Employment Report 2024 revealed something that should stop everyone: the proportion of educated young Indians who are unemployed doubled from 35 percent in 2000 to 66 percent in 2022. That was before the current wave of AI automation hit its stride.

We educated a generation for jobs that are now being automated. And we are educating the next generation for the same jobs. The college that is still teaching the curriculum of 2015 is a factory producing workers for a world that no longer exists.

WHAT ACTUALLY PROTECTS YOU

The uncle does not warn and walk away.

There is a version of your career that survives this. There is a version that thrives. But it requires you to stop thinking about your job description and start thinking about your irreplaceability.

The question to ask yourself is not: can AI do any part of my job? The answer to that is almost certainly yes. The question is: what part of my job can AI not do — and am I deliberately building my career around that part?

AI handles execution. It will increasingly handle analysis. It will never handle human accountability, contextual judgment in relationships, creative insight that connects to cultural and emotional truth, or the trust that accumulates between people over years of shared experience. These are not soft skills. They are the hardest skills. They take the longest to build. And they are the least automatable things a professional can offer.

The marketing manager who becomes a brand strategist — who can read a cultural moment and position a brand within it in a way no algorithm trained on past data can predict — is not replaceable. The accountant who becomes a business advisor, who understands what the numbers mean about the company's future and can guide a client through a difficult decision, is not replaceable. The lawyer who builds the client relationships that mean people call them when the problem is so complex and high-stakes that no AI can be trusted with it — that lawyer is not replaceable.

The key insight is simple: the value used to be in knowing things and doing things. AI knows more than you and can do more of the work than you. The new value is in being trusted, being accountable, and being the human in the room when the decision matters.

And here is the one practical thing to carry out of this chapter: the most powerful position in the next five years will belong to the person who can work with AI at expert level. Not use it casually. Not know its name. Use it at expert level — who knows how to direct it, check it, combine its output with human judgment, and take ownership of the result. That person will be ten times more productive than the person who ignores AI and five times more valuable than the person who only uses it casually.

The window to become that person is open right now. It will not stay open.

THE DOOR BEHIND YOU

That choice — to build toward judgment and irreplaceability, or to keep doing what you have always done and hope the wave passes — belongs to you.

But the wave is not only approaching professionals who work for companies. We have spent this chapter talking about people who have a manager above them, a team below them, a salary arriving each month, and the assumption that the organisation they work for will continue to exist and continue to need them.

What about the people who built the organisation? The ones who took the risk, signed the rent agreement, hired the people, lay awake at three in the morning worrying about payroll? The business owners. The entrepreneurs. The men and women who spent years building something that employs other people.

They are not immune. They are facing a different terror. Not the terror of losing a job — but the terror of watching something you built become obsolete, or of trying to adopt a technology you do not fully understand fast enough to survive competitors who have nothing to lose.

I have sat in rooms with these people. I know what they are afraid of. Some of them are afraid of exactly the right things and do not know where to start. Some of them are adopting AI frantically, without a clear strategy, spending money they cannot afford on tools they do not understand. And some of them — more than you would expect — are simply frozen. Watching the wave and unable to move.

The employee watches the wave and worries about their job. The business owner watches the wave and worries about everything — their business, their employees, their years of investment, and whether the life they built is going to survive what is coming.

That is the next chapter.

The professional fears losing a salary. The businessman fears losing a life's work. These are not the same fear. The employee's terror arrives in a meeting, in a redundancy letter, in a hiring freeze. The businessman's terror arrives in a different way — in a client who says the competitor is now using AI and their prices have dropped by forty percent. In a product that took two years to build and six months to become obsolete. In a team of twelve people who depend on decisions being made by a person who has never felt less certain of anything.

The uncle has sat in that room too. He knows that terror. And he has something to say to the businessman that the businessman does not expect to hear — because it is not only a warning. It is a map.

CHAPTER 10: THE TERRIFIED BUSINESSMAN

CHAPTER 10

THE TERRIFIED BUSINESSMAN

YOU BUILT SOMETHING REAL. THAT IS EXACTLY WHY YOU ARE AFRAID.

I have sat in enough rooms with enough business owners to know what this chapter is about.

The fear arrives at midnight. It comes as a WhatsApp message you did not send but almost did, to someone you trust, asking a question you are not ready to ask out loud. It comes as a browser tab open to an article about AI that you closed before finishing because the implications were too large to sit with at that hour. The phone on the nightstand. The ceiling in the dark. The numbers that still work, for now, and the feeling that the ground beneath them is shifting in a way you cannot quite name.

That is the fear of a person who built something — with their hands, their savings, their reputation, and years of their life — and is now watching a threat approach that does not announce itself. Not a competitor you can name. Not a market shift you can track on a graph. Something that is changing the rules of the game while the game is still being played.

Most are standing still. The stillness feels like dignity. Moving feels like panic. And panic, they have always believed, is the enemy of good decision-making.

But the wave does not respect the distinction between panic and courage. It arrives either way.

So let me say, clearly, before anything else: if you are a business owner and you are afraid, your fear is correct. Your instinct is right. The threat is real. The question is not whether you should be afraid. The question is what you do with that fear in the next twelve months.

ONE PERSON. ONE BILLION DOLLARS. NO EMPLOYEES.

In early 2024, Sam Altman — the CEO of OpenAI, the company that built ChatGPT — was in conversation with Alexis Ohanian, the co-founder of Reddit. The conversation was casual. Altman was speculating, almost offhandedly, about something his circle of tech CEO friends had been discussing.

He said: "In my little group chat with my tech CEO friends there's this betting pool for the first year that there is a one-person billion-dollar company — which would have been unimaginable without AI — and now it will happen."

Read that again, slowly.

One person. One billion dollars. No team, no departments, no HR, no office — one person with AI as their entire organisation. Altman was not trying to frighten anyone. He was sharing a fact the way you share a weather forecast. Sunny tomorrow. Also: the structure of business is about to change completely.

The startup world buzzed. LinkedIn posts were written. Podcasts celebrated the dawn of the solopreneur.

Here is the implication that nobody was writing LinkedIn posts about.

If one person with AI can build a billion-dollar company, then one person with AI can also replicate your company. Study your business, automate your processes, undercut your prices, and compete with you using less than ten percent of the people you employ. Every business you have built, every market you have served, every advantage you believed was yours — all of it is now within reach of a single smart person with the right AI tools and a clear-eyed look at what you do.

That is what the Altman quote actually means for the business owner who has been in the market for fifteen years. Not inspiration. Warning.

EVERY BUSINESS HAS SEVEN VERTICALS. AI IS COMING FOR ALL OF THEM.

Every business — whether it is a manufacturing company in Pune, a trading house in Ahmedabad, a garment exporter in Surat, or a professional services firm in Bengaluru — runs on seven functions. These are not optional. They are the bones of any organisation.

Sales. Marketing. Finance. Human Resources. Operations. Research and Development. Management.

Every rupee you have invested, every person you have hired, every system you have built exists within one of these seven functions. Your business is, at its core, a machine made of these seven parts working together.

Now here is the truth that should make you put down this book and think.

AI is automating all seven. Not eventually. Now. At different speeds, at different levels of completeness, but the direction is not in question. Sales automation already exists — AI tools that prospect, outreach, qualify, and follow up without a human initiating each step. Marketing automation already exists — AI that writes campaigns, generates content, places ads, and optimises spend in real time. Finance automation already exists — AI that closes books, processes invoices, detects anomalies, and forecasts cash flow. HR automation already exists — AI that screens candidates, processes paperwork, and handles routine employee queries. Operations automation is well underway — AI that manages inventory, predicts maintenance needs, and optimises supply chains. Even R&D is being changed — AI that accelerates research, designs experiments, and identifies patterns in data no human team could process in time.

And Management? AI that analyses performance data, flags risks, summarises reports, drafts decisions for review, and coordinates between functions — that too exists, and is developing faster than any of the others.

• • •

On February 17, 2026 — three days before this book went to print — Vinod Khosla, the founder of Khosla Ventures and co-founder of Sun Microsystems, stood at the India AI Impact Summit in New Delhi and said something that every Indian business owner needs to hear.

He said: "By 2030, there will be no such thing as IT services. There will be no such thing as BPO. Those are gone."

He did not say this to an audience of alarmists or activists. He said it at the largest AI summit ever held in the Global South, in front of more than three lakh attendees, business leaders, government ministers, and the heads of the world's most powerful AI companies. He said it plainly, on the record, knowing it would be reported. He added: "In the next five years, AI will be better than most humans at most things. There's very little where humans will be substantially better."

This is not a foreign warning about a distant market. This is a man who has built and funded some of the world's most consequential technology companies, speaking in Delhi, about India, to Indians, about what is coming for the economy that you have built your business inside.

The seven verticals of your business are not abstract. They are where your people sit, where your costs live, and where your competitors are now pointing their AI tools. If Khosla is right — and the evidence of the last three years suggests he is directionally correct — then the question is not whether your business will be affected. It is whether you are the one doing the disrupting or the one being disrupted.

• • •

In every presentation I give to business leaders, I tell them the same thing: your company currently runs on seven verticals. Make AI the eighth. Not a department. Not a pilot project. A fundamental vertical that cuts across and augments everything else. The businesses that do this will survive. The businesses that treat AI as a technology experiment will not.

Most of them nod. Almost none of them do it. And the gap between understanding and action is where businesses die.

YOUR BEST PEOPLE CAN BECOME YOUR MOST DANGEROUS COMPETITORS

There is a threat that business owners are not discussing, because it is uncomfortable to name. It sits in the office every day. It attends the weekly meetings. It knows the clients, the margins, the processes, and the gaps in your operation.

It is your senior employees.

This is not a new worry. Experienced employees leaving to start competing businesses is as old as commerce. But AI has changed the scale of what a single departing employee can do with what they know.

Consider what your sales head knows when he leaves: your client list, your pricing strategy, the objections your clients raise, the reasons they chose you, the terms you offer, and the weaknesses in your delivery. In the past, armed with that knowledge, a departing employee needed capital, a team, infrastructure, and time to build a competing operation. These were real barriers. They took years. Many people tried and failed, not for lack of knowledge, but for lack of resources.

Today, that same sales head leaves on Friday. By Sunday evening, he has asked an AI to help him build a go-to-market strategy using everything he knows about your business. By the following Friday, he has AI generating his marketing content, drafting his outreach emails to your clients, analysing his pricing position, and handling his initial sales conversations. He does not need to hire a team yet. He does not need a large office. He needs a laptop, a few AI subscriptions costing a fraction of what you pay in monthly salaries, and the domain knowledge he accumulated on your payroll.

That ex-sales head is not copying you with ten people. He is copying you with AI. And he can price below you, because his cost structure is a fraction of yours.

This is not hypothetical. This is happening in every industry where knowledge is the primary asset — which, in the modern economy, is most industries.

The business that once had its advantage woven into its structure — into its accumulated processes, its client relationships, its institutional knowledge held by ten people who had been there since the beginning — now has an advantage that a single AI-equipped person can reverse-engineer in a weekend. The connective tissue of your business, the knowledge that held it together, can now walk out the door in one person's head and be rebuilt in days.

Every senior employee in your organisation is a potential founder of your most dangerous competitor. This is not a reason to distrust your people. It is a reason to ask yourself: is your business's advantage so embedded in your AI systems, your data, and your accumulated institutional intelligence that it cannot simply walk out the door in a person's head?

If the answer is no — if your advantage lives primarily in the knowledge of your people rather than in systems and data that belong to the organisation — then you are more vulnerable than you think.

YOU HAVE MORE DATA THAN YOU KNOW. YOU ARE USING ALMOST NONE OF IT.

In every conversation I have with business owners about AI, the moment I mention data, I see the same expression. They assume they understand what I mean. They have spreadsheets. They have an ERP system. They have sales reports. They have data.

They do not understand what I mean.

Data is not what you see on the screen. Data is every signal your business generates, at every level of its operation — most of which you are currently ignoring because you have never had the tools to capture or interpret it. The temperature on your factory floor. The time between a customer query and your team's response. The pattern of which invoices get paid late and by whom. The sequence of steps your best salesperson takes before closing a deal. The difference in output between your morning shift and your afternoon shift. The noise pattern of a machine before it breaks down.

Take that last one: which invoices get paid late and by whom. A business that captures this data and feeds it into an AI model predicts, months in advance, which clients are likely to default. It stops extending credit to those clients before the crisis arrives. It redirects its collection efforts to exactly the right accounts at exactly the right moment. This is not a technology experiment. It is the difference between a company that manages cash flow and a company that predicts it. Most businesses in India are still managing. Their competitors who are embedding AI are beginning to predict.

Your competitors who are embedding AI into their operations are building a data advantage — an accumulating, compounding intelligence about their business that grows more valuable every day. The business that captures and learns from data at this level of granularity will make better decisions faster, waste less, serve customers more precisely, and identify problems before they become crises.

The business that is still looking at monthly Excel reports is not competing on the same terms. It is not even playing the same game.

THE ROOM WHERE NO ONE SAYS WHAT THEY KNOW

A business owner has called his senior team together to discuss AI. He has read enough to know it is important. He is worried. Around the table sit people who have been with the company for ten, fifteen, twenty years. The general manager of operations. The finance head. The senior sales director. These are people whose judgment the owner trusts and whose institutional knowledge he depends on.

A younger voice at the table — perhaps someone from the technology team, perhaps an eager manager in their early thirties — raises what is actually the most important point of the meeting. Something specific about how AI could change a core process. Something that reflects a genuine understanding of what is coming.

One of the senior figures leans back slightly. A small exhale. Not quite a laugh. “I’ve been doing this for twenty years,” he says. Pause. “We tried something like this. In 2015.” He does not finish the sentence. He does not need to. The room already knows what the unfinished sentence means. The owner nods slowly. The younger voice does not speak again. Someone asks about the Q3 numbers. The meeting moves on. Nothing is decided.

The owner does not intervene. He uses the senior figure's resistance as permission to defer a decision he does not yet know how to make.

I have seen this meeting in manufacturing companies and trading houses, and professional services firms. I have seen it happen with intelligent, successful people who built real businesses through genuine hard work. And I want to say, with as much respect as I can carry, that this meeting is where businesses begin to die.

Seniority, in every organisation before AI, was built on experience. The person who had seen more was more valuable than the person who had seen less. This made complete sense. Experience was the best available proxy for judgment. And then AI arrived and changed what experience means.

A two-year-experienced AI engineer who deeply understands these tools and their implications knows something about the future of your business that your twenty-year general manager does not. Not because the engineer is more intelligent or more committed. But because experience in the AI era is measured differently. What you have seen is less important than what the technology can now do. And the technology is moving faster than any career can track.

The senior manager who dismisses the AI conversation is not doing so out of malice. He is doing so out of fear — the same fear the owner feels. But where the owner's fear is quiet and private, the senior manager's fear has found a socially acceptable costume: authority. His seniority gives him the right to declare the threat unreal. And the owner, who does not yet fully understand the technology himself, does not have the confidence to challenge that authority.

So the young voice goes silent. The room moves on. And somewhere outside, a smarter, leaner, AI-equipped competitor is beginning to solve the problem your company just declined to address.

THE PARALYSIS THAT LOOKS LIKE PRUDENCE

Here is what I know about you, if you are a business owner reading this chapter.

You know the threat is real. You have known it for a while. You have heard the presentations, read the articles, perhaps sat in a session or two about AI adoption. You can talk about it intelligently in a conversation. You know the names of the tools. You have probably asked your team to "look into it" at some point.

And then nothing happened. Or something small happened — a pilot project, a tool that someone in marketing started using, a chatbot on the website — and you told yourself you had begun. But the core of the business, the processes and structures and decision-making systems that make the company what it is, those have not changed.

You are not unusual. A 2025 World Trade Organization and International Chamber of Commerce survey found that only 41 percent of small businesses have adopted AI, compared to more than 60 percent of large firms. And within small businesses, the gap is widening: growing SMEs are adopting AI aggressively, while stagnant ones are watching. The technology is not the divide. The willingness to act is the divide.

Why the paralysis? I have heard every version of the reason. The investment is unclear. The technology is changing too fast to commit. My industry is different. My customers are not ready. My team does not have the skills. I need to find the right person first. I am waiting for the right moment.

These are real concerns. They are not excuses. They reflect genuine uncertainty in a genuinely uncertain landscape.

But here is a different frame.

The right moment to begin adopting AI in your business was two years ago. The second-best moment is today. And the moment after today will be more expensive, more difficult, and more dangerous than today — because every day your competitor who has already begun is compounding their advantage over you. Waiting for certainty in an uncertain landscape is not prudence. It is a choice to fall further behind while feeling responsible about it.

Every business owner I have spoken to knows that what I have just said is true. The knowledge is not the problem. The problem is the gap between knowing and acting. And that gap, in most cases, is fear. Not the fear of failure — business owners are comfortable with failure, they have navigated it before. It is the fear of a specific kind of incompetence: the fear of investing in something you do not fully understand, in a direction you cannot fully predict, with consequences that affect the people who depend on you.

This fear is honourable. It comes from the same place as the responsibility that made you a good business owner.

But it will not save your business.

WHAT THIS BOOK IS ASKING YOU TO DO

This book has spent nine chapters talking about what is being lost. About the workers who are unwarned. About the professionals who believe they are safe. At every point, it has tried to tell the truth about the scale and speed of what is coming.

Now let me be clear about what is being asked of you.

Not to understand AI completely before you act. Nobody does. The people who built the most successful technology companies of the last twenty years did not wait for complete understanding before they moved. They moved, they learned, they corrected.

Not to bet the company on a single transformation. To begin. Seriously begin. Not a pilot project that sits in a corner of the marketing department. A fundamental question, asked honestly, about which of your seven business functions is most exposed to AI disruption — and therefore most urgently in need of AI investment. And then a real commitment to beginning there.

To create space in your organisation for the voices that understand this technology, even if those voices are younger and less experienced in your industry than the voices you currently trust. Seniority built your company. But seniority, alone, will not navigate what is coming.

And to do something that may be the hardest thing on this list: to name the fear. Not to your investors or your board, but to yourself. To say: I am afraid of this. I do not fully understand it. But I know it is real, and I know that doing nothing is the most dangerous choice available to me.

The business owners who act from that honest place — who stop performing confidence they do not have and start building the knowledge they need — are the ones who will find a path through.

Because the wave will not stop. But the person who turns to face it, who learns to read it and move with it rather than stand paralysed before it, has a chance. A real chance. Not guaranteed, but real.

Your terror is correct. Your business is at risk. Every non-AI business will be disrupted. The only question is whether you are the one doing the disrupting – of your own company, deliberately, on your own terms – or whether someone else does it to you, without warning, before you are ready.

The next chapter will not add to your fear. It is the chapter about what you can actually do. The tools available, the approaches that work for businesses at your scale, and the specific opportunities that this wave, as disruptive as it is, has placed within reach of the person willing to move.

The uncle did not warn you to leave you in the dark. He warned you so you would have time to prepare.

Come.

CHAPTER 11: A WALK THROUGH TOMORROW

CHAPTER 11

A WALK THROUGH TOMORROW

EVERY PROBLEM YOU LIVE WITH IS A BUSINESS WAITING TO BE BUILT.

I want to begin this chapter with a dog.

His name was Troy. A Siberian Husky. My Siberian Husky. And I am going to ask you to bear with me for a moment, because I am still grieving him two years later and this is the chapter about solutions and hope, and Troy is the best explanation of both that I have.

Troy loved walks. Loved them the way only a dog can — with his entire being, from his ears to his tail, from the moment the idea entered his head to the moment his paws hit the footpath. But I could not take him every day. My schedule did not allow it. It was mainly on holidays and free mornings that we went out together.

Now here is the peculiar thing. Troy always knew when we were going for a walk.

Not when I told him. Before I told him. He would be at the door, ready, tail moving like a ceiling fan on full speed, before I had said a single word or made a single obvious gesture. I wore the same clothes to the gym. I left the house for meetings and dinners just as often. But Troy never got up for those. Only for the walk. Every time.

I thought about this for a long time. How did he know?

The answer, I eventually understood, was data. Not data in the way we usually think of it — not spreadsheets and reports. Data in its truest sense: every small signal the world around him was sending, all at once, combined into a pattern that his brain had quietly learned over months.

He slept late. My phone was not ringing with work calls. The television had been on for a while. It was a Sunday or a holiday. The time was right. The mood in the house was unhurried. Combine all of that with my body language, my choice of shoes, the way I picked up the leash even before I consciously decided to reach for it — and Troy had already solved the problem. He was not guessing. He was pattern-matching with sensors I did not even know I was broadcasting.

In the wild, animals do this to survive. The predator reads a thousand tiny signals before it moves. The prey reads a thousand signals before it runs. Life depends on the accuracy of the reading.

AI has given humans that same capability. Not just to read patterns — but to read patterns at a scale, a speed, and a level of granularity that no human brain, however brilliant, can match alone. Troy's skill, applied to your home, your city, your business, your country. That is what this chapter is about.

I am going to walk you through my day. From my living room to my bathroom to my car to the streets of Mumbai. At every step, I am going to show you what already exists, what is coming soon, and — most importantly — where the opportunity sits for a young, smart, curious person who is paying attention.

THE AIR CONDITIONER THAT ARGUES WITH NO ONE

I am sitting in my living room as I write this. The air conditioner has been running for three years without being switched off. There is a reason for that, which I will save for later. But right now I want to ask you a simple question about this air conditioner, or about any air conditioner in any home you have ever lived in.

Why, on the same temperature setting, do you sometimes feel cold and sometimes feel warm?

You know the answer instinctively, even if you have never put it into words. More people in the room. Outside temperature has changed. Humidity. Whether you have just eaten, or just exercised, or just come in from the rain. The sun hitting one wall of the room differently in the afternoon than in the morning. A dozen variables, all changing simultaneously, and your one air conditioner sitting there doing the same thing it did two hours ago because nobody has told it anything different.

In my home, the primary casualty of this situation is my marriage.

My wife Sana runs cold. I run warm. At night, this creates a negotiation that would exhaust the most experienced diplomats. She lowers the temperature. I survive. Then at 2am, the recycled air has settled over her like a second blanket she did not ask for, and she wakes with cold arms and the particular irritation of someone whose sleep has been interrupted by a machine that does not know her. She raises the temperature. I wake overheated. She lowers it again before I notice. I pull the blanket. She pushes it off. Somewhere around 4am we achieve an uneasy truce and by 6am the alarm goes off and we begin the whole performance again.

This is not a small problem. This is a nightly event in tens of millions of Indian homes. It is, in the language of business, a large and underserved market.

Now imagine a different system.

Thermal sensors in the living room and the bedroom that track each person's body heat individually. A humidity sensor. A sensor for outside temperature, updated live. Sensors on the walls that measure how much heat the building itself has absorbed during the day. Individual body temperature readings, available through a simple wearable or even a phone. Motion detectors that know who is in the room and where.

Connect all of this to a single AI that watches, learns, and adjusts. For one week, let the family use everything normally — change the AC as they please, switch lights on and off, adjust the fan. The AI watches and records every correction. Then, carefully, it begins to make its own adjustments. Small ones at first. It tests. It learns from your corrections. If you change what it did, it notes that. If you leave it alone, it notes that too.

After a few weeks, something remarkable happens. Sana stops waking up at 2am. I stop kicking off the blanket. The system has learned, at the level of individual people in a specific room in a specific building in a specific city, what comfort actually means.

Not the manufacturer's default. Not the average. Not a compromise. The actual, personalised, continuously improving answer.

No one touches a button. The system does it.

This is not science fiction. Every component I just described exists today. The sensors are cheap. The AI learning systems are available. What does not yet exist is someone who has put all of it together into a product designed for the Indian home, sold and installed and supported as a complete system. That someone could be you.

And that is before we even talk about what this system learns about your electricity bill, your appliance lifetimes, your air quality, and the pattern of your daily life that emerges when you watch a home intelligently for long enough.

THE BATHROOM THAT WOKE ME UP

Sana, who is an intelligent and resourceful woman despite what the air conditioner dispute might suggest, decided to solve our bathroom problem with technology.

The problem was simple: she likes all six bathroom lights on at all times. I, when I visit the bathroom at night, want complete darkness. Complete darkness is not a preference. It is a survival strategy. If I see light, my brain decides it is morning and begins composing emails. I need to return to sleep immediately. I need zero stimulation.

Sana installed a motion sensor. For all the lights.

I now emerge from the bathroom at 2am like a man who has been struck by a spotlight, wide awake, blinking at the ceiling, composing emails.

Automation has made my problem worse. This is what happens when you automate without personalising. A motion sensor does not know who has walked in. It knows only that someone has walked in. It responds identically to Sana at 8pm and to me at 2am, because it cannot tell us apart. This is not intelligence. This is a switch with extra steps.

Real intelligence would do something different.

A thermal sensor on the door recognises, by body heat pattern and height and movement signature, who has entered. It has already learned, over weeks, that this particular person at this particular hour wants no lights and perhaps the faintest nightlight near the floor. It has learned that the other person, at any hour, prefers full brightness and warm-toned light. The bathroom prepares itself before the person has crossed the threshold.

The same system knows, because it is connected to the same sensor network as the rest of the house, that it is Tuesday, a working day, that one person's alarm is set for 5:45am, and that the shower should be at 42 degrees — because it is January, because the outside temperature last night dropped to 19 degrees, because that is what that person chose on the eleven previous January mornings when the temperature was in this range.

Sana likes her water at a temperature that I can only describe as optimistic. I like mine hot enough to feel alive. The geyser knows this. It has already prepared both.

On the morning of a 5am flight — and I take several flights a week, so the calendar knows which mornings these are — the geyser began heating forty-five minutes earlier than usual. Nobody set an alarm for the geyser. Nobody programmed a special profile. The system read the pattern: this person, on mornings with very early flight departures, showers twenty minutes earlier. It adjusted. Silently. This is the difference between automation and intelligence — one follows instructions, the other anticipates needs.

This is a multi-crore business. Not one product — a system. Sensors, learning software, installation, calibration, maintenance, and the network effect that makes every home smarter as more homes join. The company that builds this for the Indian market, designed for Indian homes, Indian family structures, Indian weather patterns, and the particular chaos of Indian morning routines, will not struggle for customers.

Sana, for the record, remains responsible for the motion sensor situation. The AI can fix many things. Spousal decisions made without consultation remain outside its scope.

THE CAR THAT KNOWS MUMBAI BETTER THAN I DO

I take a couple of flights every week. I have businesses and assignments that pull me in multiple directions across the city. I hate being late with the particular hatred of a person who is late often enough to have developed strong feelings about it.

My solution, which is not a good solution, is to leave absurdly early. I arrive at the airport with time to spare, sit in a lounge I do not enjoy, and feel irritated at myself for having over-corrected. Then the next week, running late from a meeting, I do not leave early enough and sit in traffic composing the apology I am about to give at the check-in counter.

There is no middle ground when the variable — Mumbai traffic — is as unpredictable as the weather and twice as personal.

Everyone tells me self-driving cars will never work in Mumbai. The traffic is too complex. The rules are guidelines rather than laws. The cows wandering across dividers, the hand-carts materialising from side lanes, the auto-rickshaws that treat lane markings as a suggestion best considered and then dismissed — this, people tell me, is too much for any machine to navigate.

I disagree completely.

AI does not need simple conditions. AI needs data. The more complex the environment, the more data it generates, and the smarter the system becomes. Mumbai traffic is not an obstacle to self-driving vehicles. Mumbai traffic is the world's most demanding training ground. The system that learns to navigate Grant Road on a Friday evening will have no difficulty with any road anywhere else on the planet.

Self-driving cars are coming to Mumbai. Not because someone decided Mumbai was ready. Because AI learns until it is ready, and Mumbai will simply make it learn faster.

But my real interest is in what happens when every car on the road is talking to every other car.

Not in the distant future. Right now, the early version of this is already being built. It is called V2X — vehicle to everything communication. Your car talks to the traffic signal, to the car in front, to the car behind, to the city's traffic management system, all simultaneously, all in real time. Globally, this technology is already being deployed in highways and smart cities. China has more than 700,000 kilometres of V2X-enabled roads. The United States has mandated it for new vehicles. India will follow, not in decades, in years.

When every car knows where every other car is going, what changes?

Everything.

Traffic is, at its heart, a coordination problem. Ten thousand individual drivers making individual decisions, none of whom can see more than a few cars ahead, none of whom know what is happening three intersections away. This is why traffic jams form and cascade and last for hours after the original problem has resolved. The system has no intelligence. It is ten thousand people guessing.

Now give the system intelligence. Let every car share its destination, its urgency, its route. Let a central AI assign priority dynamically, like an air traffic controller who can see every aircraft simultaneously. The car that is rushing to a hospital moves first. The car whose occupant has a flexible schedule, and is offered a small payment to yield priority, falls back. No sirens. No manual intervention. A market of movement, clearing itself in real time.

I am willing to pay five hundred rupees to reach the airport thirty minutes faster. Somewhere in the same traffic, someone not in a hurry would accept five hundred rupees to let me through. The system connects us, executes the transaction, and adjusts our routes in seconds. This will happen. The only question is who builds it first.

In India. For India. Understanding Indian traffic, Indian pricing, Indian behaviour. The founder of that company is reading this book right now. I am reasonably confident of this.

THE SIGNAL THAT DOESN'T KNOW IT'S 3AM

A quick fact for readers outside Mumbai: travelling ten kilometres inside the city can take two hours on a bad day. I visit my factory, which is within the Mumbai Metropolitan Region, on certain days. Door to door, one way, is sometimes three hours. On a factory visit day, I spend six hours of my life in a car. There are people who do this every day.

Here is a more absurd fact: many of those traffic signals are running on the same timer at 3am as they were at 9am. Red for sixty seconds. Green for sixty seconds. The road is empty. A single car sits waiting at a red light at 3am, obeying a system that was calibrated for rush hour, in the dark, with no one watching. Then, because the junction is empty and dark and the signal cycle is too long, a driver coming from the other direction decides the red is not worth respecting. That is when accidents happen.

This is, honestly, one of the easiest problems on this list to solve. And I want to say something directly to any policy maker who is reading this book.

I will architect this solution for Mumbai. Free of cost. No fee. No obligation. Simply because I want my city to work better and I believe I can help it do so.

The model is this. Install cameras, the kind that already exist for traffic violation detection, on the approach roads to every major signal. Not just at the signal itself, but further back, so the system can see what is coming before it arrives. Connect those cameras to a simple AI that reads traffic volume, vehicle types, and movement patterns.

Give every traffic constable at that junction a simple device with one button. Press the button when you want the signal to change to the next pattern. Nothing more complicated than that. The constable does not program anything. He does not learn software. He makes one decision, as he has always made, and presses one button. The AI watches what he does and records it: what did the camera see, what time was it, what day was it, what was the traffic doing, and what did the constable decide?

Over weeks, the system learns the constable's judgment. It learns that on Tuesday mornings between 9 and 10, when the school bus is visible on the approach road, he always holds the green for ten extra seconds. It learns that after 11pm, he shortens the red cycle because the road is clearing. It learns the difference between a normal Tuesday and a Tuesday before a public holiday.

Then, gradually, the system begins operating autonomously. The constable is still there. He can override at any moment. But the routine decisions, the ones that follow a pattern the machine has now understood better than any individual human can, those happen automatically.

Connect all the signals in the city to a central system, and the signals begin coordinating with each other. A green wave down a main artery at 8am. A clearing cycle across a neighbourhood at midnight. The city breathing, intelligently, rather than pulsing on timers set in 2009.

Bengaluru attempted a version of this in 2023. Signal wait times dropped 17 percent before the project stalled on implementation. The model stalled because it tried to replace the human rather than learn from him. Keeping the constable in the loop is not a compromise. It is why the model works.

THE CONSTABLE WHO KNOWS THINGS THE CAMERA DOESN'T

Let me say something that surprises people when I say it: the traffic constable is not the problem. He is, in many ways, part of the solution.

In Mumbai, you will see something that makes no sense to anyone visiting from another country. The traffic signal is working. It is green, it is red, it is doing its job. And standing next to it is a traffic constable, manually directing traffic. Both systems operating simultaneously. One electronic, one human, each apparently unaware that the other exists.

A few metres away, cars are double-parked. A delivery van has stopped at a corner. An auto-rickshaw has created an improvised third lane. The signal is managing the intersection. The constable is managing the signal. Nobody is managing the chaos thirty metres back that is the actual source of the jam.

What if the constable did not stand at the signal at all?

The signal, connected to the AI system we just described, does not need him there. It is handling the intersection. What it cannot do is walk. It cannot move to where the problem is. It cannot stand in the middle of a clogged side street and wave one lane through. It cannot walk up to the delivery driver and explain, firmly, why double-parking at this particular corner backs up traffic all the way to the next intersection.

The constable can.

Now give him the device he already has — the internet-connected tablet for checking documents and issuing fines — and add to it a live feed from the city's traffic AI. The system knows, from cameras and vehicle data and historical patterns, that a problem is beginning to form two streets over. It tells the constable, specifically, where to go. Not after the jam has formed. Before it forms. He walks over, clears the issue, and the downstream cascade never happens.

Allow drivers to report problems too. A simple flag in the map application. That report feeds the AI. The constable gets directed. The system learns which kinds of reports are reliable and which are not, and it weights them accordingly over time.

The constable is not replaced. He is given intelligence. He goes from reacting to problems he can see to preventing problems the system can see coming. His effectiveness multiplies. The same number of constables, doing a different job, covering more ground, with better information.

I believe, and I will stand by this number, that the two systems together — intelligent signals and AI-guided constables — can reduce Mumbai's traffic congestion by twenty percent. That is not a small number. That is hours returned to millions of people every single day.

EVERY PROBLEM IS A BUSINESS

I have walked you from my bedroom to my bathroom to my car to the streets of my city.

Troy taught me something on all those walks. He did not wait for someone to explain the walk to him. He read the signals. He understood the pattern. And when the moment arrived, he was already at the door.

Every problem I described in this chapter is real. The AC that does not know who is in the room. The bathroom that cannot tell the difference between the person who wants darkness and the person who wants a lit-up spa. The car sitting in traffic that has no idea what is happening at the next intersection. The signal running on a 2009 timer at 3am on an empty road. The constable standing next to a working signal instead of standing where the problem actually is.

These are not complaints. These are specifications.

The sensors are available. The AI platforms are available. The cloud infrastructure is available. What is not yet available is the person who looks at these problems and sees not inconvenience but opportunity. That person does not need to be a software engineer. They need to understand the problem, find the engineers who can build the solution, and have the courage to begin. The knowledge of what is possible is no longer locked inside research labs and technology companies. It is available, right now, to anyone willing to learn how to use it.

This book has spent ten chapters describing what is being lost. Jobs that will disappear. Industries that will compress. Professionals who believe they are safe and are not. Business owners who know the wave is coming and cannot make themselves move.

This chapter is for the person who reads all of that and asks the different question: where is the opportunity in this?

The answer is: everywhere you look. Every system that serves people badly, every daily frustration that millions of people share, every process that still runs on human judgment that could be learned and automated – each one is a gap. Each gap is a market. Each market is a company waiting to be founded by someone who arrives at the door before anyone else realises the walk has begun.

Troy always knew. He was at the door.

Be at the door.

CHAPTER 12: A WALK THROUGH TOMORROW

CHAPTER 12

WAKE UP

I AM NOT ANGRY WITH ANYONE. I AM ANGRY AT THE SILENCE.

Let me show you the full picture.

For eleven chapters, I have taken you through one sector at a time. The security guard. The farm labourer. The garment stitcher. The delivery boy. The construction worker. The call centre agent. The professional who uses ChatGPT and believes that makes him safe. The business owner who is frozen between knowing and acting.

I did it that way deliberately. Because the moment you see the full number all at once, the mind does something that protects it from the weight — it becomes abstract. It becomes a statistic. And statistics do not wake people up. People wake people up.

So I showed you people first. Rajan on the bike. The woman whose hands have stitched ten thousand times today. The guard at the gate who has never heard of a facial recognition camera. The delivery boy training his own replacement with every route he rides.

Now I am going to show you the number.

SECTOR	WORKERS AT RISK	TIMELINE	WHAT IS REPLACING THEM
Security & Surveillance	9–12 million	Now	AI cameras, facial recognition, remote monitoring
Agriculture (labourers)	144 million landless; 600 million dependent	5–15 years	Planting & harvesting robots, mandi algorithm
Garments & Textiles	20–27 million (of 45 million total)	Now–2032	Sewbots, AI cutting, mass customisation, reshoring
Logistics, Delivery & Gig	12 million today; 23.5 million by 2030	3–7 years	Drones, autonomous delivery, dark store robots
Construction	70 million workers	5–10 years	Prefab, bricklaying robots, 3D printing, autonomous excavators
BPO & Call Centres	5.4 million direct; 15 million+ indirect	Now–2027	AI voice agents, chatbots, automated back offices
White Collar & Professional	50 million+ knowledge workers	2–5 years	AI copilots replacing entry-level roles across all functions
Retail, Healthcare Support, Education & Domestic Workers	40–60 million	Underway	Quick commerce, AI tutors, automation of support roles
TOTAL EXPOSURE – THIS EDITION	300–400 million people	Within one generation	The largest silent displacement in human history

Security & 9–12 million Now AI cameras, facial Surveillance recognition, remote monitoring

Agriculture 144 million 5–15 years Planting & harvesting (labourers) landless; 600 robots, mandi million algorithm dependent

Garments & Textiles 20–27 million Now–2032 Sewbots, AI cutting, (of 45 million mass customisation, total) reshoring

Logistics, Delivery 12 million 3–7 years Drones, autonomous & Gig today; 23.5 delivery, dark store million by 2030 robots

Construction 70 million 5–10 years Prefab, bricklaying workers robots, 3D printing, autonomous excavators

BPO & Call Centres 5.4 million Now–2027 AI voice agents, direct; 15 chatbots, automated million+ back offices indirect

White Collar & 50 million+ 2–5 years AI copilots replacing Professional knowledge entry-level roles workers across all functions

Retail, Healthcare 40–60 million Underway Quick commerce, AI Support, Education & tutors, automation of Domestic Workers support roles

TOTAL EXPOSURE – THIS EDITION

300–400 million people

Within one generation

The largest silent displacement in human history

A note on the numbers: This edition covers the sectors researched for this volume. India's full exposure — including domestic workers, healthcare, retail and the informal economy in its entirety — will be examined in the next edition. The total, when complete, approaches half a billion.

Between 300 and 400 million people in India face displacement or severe income compression from AI and automation within one generation. This is not a sector problem. This is a civilisational moment.

To put that number in context: it is larger than the entire population of the United States. It is larger than the combined populations of France, Germany, the United Kingdom, and Italy. It is more than the total number of people who were displaced by any war, famine, or natural disaster in recorded human history.

And almost none of them know it is coming.

THE SILENCE THAT MADE THIS BOOK NECESSARY

I have been in business and technology in India for decades. I have watched every wave arrive. The computer. The internet. Mobile. E-commerce. Each time, there were people who saw it coming. Each time, the people who would be most affected learned last.

But this wave is different in a specific, important way.

Every previous wave created more jobs than it destroyed, eventually. The textile mill reduced hand-weavers, but it created factory workers, logistics workers, retail workers, and an entire ecosystem of new roles. The internet reduced travel agents and newspaper classifieds, but it created digital marketers, software engineers, content creators, and platform workers. You could argue, and many did, that the displaced would find new work. The argument was painful for the people experiencing the displacement, but it was not entirely wrong.

AI is different because it does not just replace a task. It replaces the category of human cognition that made the task valuable. A robot replaces a human arm. AI replaces a human brain — specifically, the parts of the brain that perform the repetitive, rule-following, pattern-matching work that makes up most jobs in every sector of every economy.

The new jobs that AI creates are jobs that require skills that take years to develop, in a system — our education system, our training infrastructure, our social safety net — that is not prepared to develop them. We are about to produce displacement at the speed of software and attempt to absorb it with the speed of a government scheme.

The gap between those two speeds is where 300 million lives will fall. That gap is what this book is about. Not the technology. Not the progress. The gap. And the silence around it.

I am not the only one saying this. And I want you to hear who else is.

In February 2026, the world's most powerful voices in technology gathered in New Delhi for the India AI Impact Summit. These are not alarmists. These are the people building the technology. This is what they said.

> *"IT and BPO services will disappear, almost certainly within the next five years. AI could eliminate large parts of white-collar employment." – Sam Altman, CEO of OpenAI, keynote address at the India AI Impact Summit, New Delhi, February 17, 2026*

> *"The man who helped build Silicon Valley warned India's biggest industry it may not exist by 2030. White-collar work – where you're sitting down at a computer, either being a lawyer or an accountant or a project manager or a marketing person – most of those tasks will be fully automated by an AI within the next 12 to 18 months." – February 2026*

> *"If we are right, by the end of 2028, more of the world's intellectual capacity could reside inside of data centers than outside of them." – Summit, New Delhi, February 19, 2026*

Altman was speaking in Delhi. India was in the room. These words were addressed to us.

Do you know what superintelligence means?

I do not mean it as a trick question. I mean it genuinely. Because Sam Altman just told a room full of the world's most powerful leaders that early versions of it could arrive within two years. And most people who read that headline moved on without fully understanding what he was describing.

Superintelligence is not a smarter version of ChatGPT. It is not a better search engine. It is not the autocomplete on your phone taken a few steps further. Superintelligence is an AI system that is capable of performing any intellectual task that a human being can perform — and then surpassing the best human performance in that task. Every task. Not just chess, which machines mastered decades ago. Not just writing code or summarising documents. But designing drugs. Running companies. Conducting scientific research. Making strategic decisions. Managing economies. Teaching. Healing. Governing.

If Altman is right — and he is the person building it, so he has more information than anyone else in that room — then by 2028, the intelligence required to do most professional work will be cheaper, faster, and more available than any human being alive.

That is what the headline means. And I believe there is an entire book waiting to be written on this question alone — what superintelligence actually is, what it means for India, and what ordinary people should understand about it before it arrives. If that is a book you want to help write, I am looking for a co-author. Reach me through Farsight Academy Press.

Nobody in power is having this conversation at the scale it deserves. Government schemes speak of skilling and reskilling as though the challenge is simply to train people for jobs that still exist. They do not ask what happens when the job category itself disappears. Industry celebrates automation as efficiency and competitiveness, which it is — but does not ask who bears the cost of that efficiency. Economists model the long-term equilibrium and assure us it will work out — but do not ask what happens to the people living in the short and medium term, which is where all of us actually live.

And the workers themselves — the guard, the stitcher, the delivery boy, the farm labourer — are going about their days, sending money home, believing that as long as they work hard and show up on time, they will be fine.

They will not be fine. Not without warning. Not without preparation. Not without someone having this conversation loudly enough that it cannot be ignored.

WHAT THE GOVERNMENT IS DOING. AND WHAT IT IS NOT.

I want to be fair.

India's government has not been idle. There are real initiatives, real investments, and real intent. I will name them honestly, because this book is not a political argument. It is a warning. And a fair warning requires a fair accounting.

Skill India Mission has trained more than 14 million people since 2015. PM MITRA textile parks are being built to modernise garment manufacturing. PLI schemes are bringing investment into electronics and manufacturing. eNAM is connecting farmers to digital markets. The Rajasthan Gig Workers Act and similar state legislation is extending protections to platform workers. NITI Aayog has published projections on the gig economy and the future of work. The government's Digital India infrastructure — UPI, Aadhaar, the JAM trinity — is genuinely world-class and has created a foundation that most countries envy.

This is real. It matters. I acknowledge it without reservation.

Now, here is what is missing.

Every one of these initiatives was designed for a pre-AI economy. Skill India trains people for jobs that exist today. It does not ask what happens when those jobs are automated in three years. PM MITRA builds parks for garment manufacturing without a plan for what happens when Sewbot economics make Indian labour uncompetitive. The gig worker welfare boards provide health insurance and accident coverage for workers in a job category that the same economy is actively building drones and robots to eliminate.

THE GOVERNMENT IS BUILDING THE SAFETY NET UNDER THE WRONG CLIFF.

What is absent is the specific, honest, public acknowledgement that AI-driven automation is coming for the largest categories of Indian employment — and a plan that begins from that acknowledgement. Not a skilling programme for today's jobs. A transition programme for tomorrow's displacement. Not a welfare board for gig workers. A conversation about what happens when the gig itself disappears.

I am not asking the government to solve an unsolvable problem. I am asking it to name the problem it has not yet named. Because the moment it names it, the nation can begin to organise around it. The silence is not protection. The silence is the danger.

WHAT I AM ASKING OF YOU

I wrote this book because I cannot stop thinking about the people at that table.

Not the numbers. The people.

The security guard who has spent eight years at the same gate, who sends Rs 18,000 home to his family in Odisha every month, who does not know that the building management committee is about to discuss a camera system at the next AGM.

The woman in Tirupur whose hands have stitched the same seam ten thousand times today, who earns Rs 9,000 a month, who has no union and no savings, who does not know that a machine called Sewbot can already do her job and that its lease cost is falling every year.

The boy from Bihar who joined Blinkit six months ago because it felt like freedom — his own schedule, his own bike, no boss standing over him — who does not know that the platform that gave him that freedom is simultaneously filing patents for the drone that will replace him.

The farmer's son, who came to the city to work construction because the farm offered nothing, who sends Rs 8,000 home and believes that India will always need builders, has never heard of a bricklaying robot or a 3D-printed house.

The marketing manager in Gurugram who uses ChatGPT every day and feels ahead of the curve, who does not know that his entry-level team — the people doing the execution work that he coordinates and supervises — are the first to disappear, and that his own role hollows from below before it reaches him.

The business owner who built something real with his hands and his years and his risk, who knows the wave is coming but cannot make himself move, who is using his senior manager's resistance as permission to defer a decision that is not deferrable.

I cannot tell each of these people what to do. Their situations are different. Their options are different. Their constraints are real and varied, and specific to them in ways I cannot fully know.

But I can tell them what is coming. And I have.

I am not angry at the technology. The technology is extraordinary. I am not angry at the companies deploying it. They are doing what companies do. I am angry at the silence. The absence of anyone saying, loudly and clearly and repeatedly: this is coming, it is coming faster than you think, and the people who will be most affected are the last to know.

That silence is what I have tried, in twelve chapters, to break.

THIS COUNTRY. THESE PEOPLE.

I love my India.

I say that not as a slogan and not as a sentiment. I say it as a fact about how I experience my life. I was born here. I built everything I have here. I have watched this country do things that should not have been possible — build a digital payments infrastructure that the United States still has not matched, land a spacecraft on the south pole of the moon, produce the largest democratic elections in human history, generate entrepreneurs and scientists and artists who have changed the world from cities and towns that the world did not notice until they did.

India has a particular genius. It is not the genius of perfect systems. We do not have perfect systems. It is the genius of people who find a way in the absence of perfect systems. The jugaad. The workaround. The person who solves the problem nobody else is even looking at. The entrepreneur who sees an opportunity in a gap that official policy has not yet noticed.

That genius will not save us from this wave automatically. Genius without warning is still caught off guard. The best swimmer in the world still drowns if he does not know there is a current until it has him.

The warning is the job of this book. I have tried to do it honestly.

What India does with the warning is not mine to dictate. I have my opinions, and I have shared them. But this country's decisions belong to its people. Everyone of them. The policymaker, the politician and the business owner and the teacher and the parent, and the young person who is reading this and asking themselves what they should do next.

I wrote this for that young person, most of all.

The one who is twenty-two years old and standing at a crossroads, trying to figure out whether to take the safe job at the company that has always existed or to build something new. The one who is looking at the problems around her — the traffic, the broken systems, the underserved needs of 1.4 billion people — and beginning, tentatively, to ask whether she could be the one to solve them.

She can.

Not despite the tsunami. Because of it. The wave that displaces will also clear the ground. The systems that are disrupted will need to be rebuilt. Gaps that automation creates in old industries will need to be filled by new ones. The people who are displaced will need to be trained, supported, retooled, and given a new purpose. Every one of those needs is a business. Every one of those businesses needs a founder.

Troy was at the door before I had consciously decided to take him for a walk. He read the signals. He understood the pattern. He was ready.

This book was the signal.

Now be at the door.

A NOTE BEFORE YOU PUT THIS BOOK DOWN

If you have read this far, you are now one of a few people in India who understands what is coming at the scale it is coming.

That is not comfortable knowledge. I know. I have been living with it for years.

But you are also now in a position that almost nobody else is in. You can see the wave. You can warn the people around you. Ask different questions in your workplace, your industry, or your family. You can look at the people who are most exposed and ask what, if anything, you can do.

You do not have to solve the whole problem. Nobody can. But you can solve the part of it that is in front of you.

That is all I was ever asking.

— Riz Thakur
Mumbai, 2026

NOTES & CITATIONS

SOURCES AND REFERENCES BY CHAPTER

The following notes list the principal sources for data, statistics, and direct quotations used throughout this book. Where possible, primary sources are cited. Secondary sources are listed where primary data was accessed through aggregated reporting. All web sources were verified as of February 2026.

PROLOGUE & INTRODUCTION

1. India's digital revolution timeline: Author's personal account, corroborated by TRAI (Telecom Regulatory Authority of India) historical bandwidth data and BSNLannual reports 1995–2005.
2. Mobile phone penetration India: TRAI Annual Reports 2000–2010; GSMA Mobile Economy India 2023.
3. ChatGPT and AI adoption India: Microsoft–LinkedIn Work Trend Index 2024; OpenAI usage data, India 2024.

CHAPTER ONE: THE MAN AT THE GATE (SECURITY & SURVEILLANCE)

1. Security industry workforce 9–12 million: NSSO 75th Round (2017–18); FICCI–PwC Security Sector Skill Council Report 2023; estimates updated via IBEF India Workforce Report 2024.
2. Agniveer scheme and military guard sector: Ministry of Defence, Agnipath Scheme notification 2022. Security sector re-absorption statistics: CAPSI (Central Association of Private Security Industry) Annual Report 2023–24.

3. 32% annual attrition in security sector: NSDC Security Sector Skill Council Survey 2023.
4. AI camera and facial recognition systems: Hikvision, Dahua, Hanwha product specifications and pricing, India market 2024. Facial recognition accuracy 99%+: NIST FRVT Ongoing Report 2024.
5. Building society technology adoption: Author's primary research; CREDAI (Confederation of Real Estate Developers' Associations of India) smart building survey 2024.
6. Surveillance camera market India: MarketsandMarkets India Video Surveillance Market Report 2024; IBEF.

CHAPTER TWO: THE PHONE IN HIS POCKET (AGRICULTURE)

1. 600 million dependent on agriculture: Census of India 2011 (most recent comprehensive census); NSSO 77th Round 2019–20; Ministry of Agriculture Annual Report 2024.
2. 144 million landless agricultural labourers: Agricultural Census of India 2015–16; NSSO Situation Assessment Survey of Agricultural Households 2019.
3. Farmer receiving 7% of consumer price: CACP (Commission for Agricultural Costs and Prices) Price Policy Reports 2022–23; NITI Aayog 'Doubling Farmers' Income' Report Vol. I–XIV.
4. Precision agriculture water reduction 90%; yield improvement 20–40%: ICAR (Indian Council of Agricultural Research) Precision Farming Annual Reports 2023; World Bank 'Digital Agriculture India' 2024.
5. eNAM reach and awareness 20–25%: Ministry of Agriculture eNAM Portal data; NABARD Rural Finance Accessibility Survey 2024.
6. Cold storage capacity 37 million metric tonnes; 35% government subsidy: National Centre for Cold-Chain Development (NCCD) Annual Report 2023–24; NHB (National Horticulture Board).
7. Agricultural drone market India growing 20% annually: DGCA drone registrations; FICCI AgriTech Report 2024.
8. Agri AI applications (crop disease detection, soil analysis): Microsoft AI for Agriculture India program documentation;

Ninjacart AI supply chain reports; Jivabhumi platform data 2024.

CHAPTER THREE: THE STITCH THAT NEVER ENDS (GARMENTS & TEXTILES)

1. 45 million garment workers in India: Ministry of Textiles Annual Report 2024–25; NSSO employment data; CITI (Confederation of Indian Textile Industry).
2. Fewer than 4% garment workers in unions: ILO Better Work India Programme 2023; AITUC garment sector survey.
3. Sewbot and automated sewing: SoftWear Automation (manufacturer of Sewbot) product documentation and published case studies 2022–24. 1 million shirts per year per Sewbot on one machine lease.
4. 80% of fashion returns due to fit: McKinsey 'The State of Fashion' 2024; Narvar Consumer Returns Report 2023.
5. 15–25% fabric waste by human cutters; <2% by AI cutting: Gerber Technology AI cutting system documentation; Lectra AutoMarker efficiency data 2024.
6. US 50% tariff on Indian goods 2025, reduced to 18%: US Trade Representative announcements; FICCI India textile trade impact assessment 2025–26. Tamil Nadu 3 million jobs threatened: Tamil Nadu government labour department report 2025.
7. Vertical farming water reduction 99%; no pesticide dependence: Plenty Inc., AeroFarms, and IIT Mumbai vertical farm pilot documentation; ICRISAT research papers.
8. Reshoring economics: BCG 'Reshoring of American Manufacturing' 2023; ITMF International Textile Manufacturing Federation cost comparison reports 2024.

CHAPTER FOUR: THE DELIVERY BOY'S LAST RIDE (LOGISTICS, DELIVERY & GIG)

1. 12 million gig workers (2024); 23.5 million projected by 2030: NITI Aayog 'India's Booming Gig and Platform Economy' 2022; Economic Survey of India 2024–25.
2. Real wages of gig workers fell 11% since 2019: ILO India Employment Report 2024; Fairwork India Rating Report 2023–24.

3. 43% of delivery workers earn under Rs 10,000/month: Centre for Sustainable Employment, Azim Premji University 'State of Working India 2023'.
4. 2.5 million orders Diwali peak: Statista India Quick Commerce Festive Season Report 2024; RedSeer estimates.
5. Amazon Prime Air, Swiggy Snacc, Zomato drone patents and testing: DGCA drone testing approvals; company public announcements and patent filings 2024–25.
6. 9 million truck drivers India: AIMTC (All India Motor Transport Congress) membership data; Ministry of Road Transport.
7. Autonomous truck technology: Torc Robotics (Daimler), TuSimple, Einride reported cost reductions 30%; industry timelines India 5–10 years: IIT Delhi Transport Research Group 2024.
8. Rajasthan Gig Workers Welfare Act 2023; Karnataka and Maharashtra equivalent legislation: State legislature acts; Fairwork India documentation.
9. Rapido motorcycle taxis and algorithm-based dispatch: Rapido platform data; KPMG India gig platform analysis 2024.

CHAPTER FIVE: THE MAN WHO LEFT THE FARM (CONSTRUCTION)

1. Construction employs 70–71 million workers: NSSO 68th Round; Ministry of Labour & Employment Annual Report 2024; NBO (National Buildings Organisation).
2. Government projection 100 million construction workers by 2030: NITI Aayog 'India's Infrastructure Vision 2030'; NIP (National Infrastructure Pipeline) employment estimates.
3. 15–20% cement and material waste on conventional sites: Confederation of Real Estate Developers (CREDAI); CII (Confederation of Indian Industry) Construction Waste Report 2023.
4. SAM (Semi-Automated Mason) bricklaying robot: Construction Robotics Inc. product documentation. 500 bricks/hour vs. 300–500 for human masons: manufacturer specifications and independent testing data.
5. 3D-printed house China, Dubai: WinSun Global case studies; ICON Inc. (US) printed construction projects; IIT Madras 3D printing pilot 2024.

6. Fastbrick Robotics Hadrian X: 1,000 bricks/hour; GPS-guided: company product documentation and media coverage.
7. PM Gati Shakti and NIP infrastructure investment: Ministry of Finance; Department for Promotion of Industry and Internal Trade (DPIIT) NIP Annual Update 2024.
8. Construction accident statistics India: NSCI (National Safety Council India) Annual Report; DGFASLI (Director General Factory Advice Service & Labour Institutes) 2023.
9. Prefabrication market India growing 15–20% annually: IBEF Construction Industry Report; Dodge Data Analytics India prefab survey 2024.

CHAPTER SIX: THE BRIDGE HAS BEEN BROKEN (BPO & CALL CENTRES)

1. TeamLease Digital / BPO hiring collapse: Reuters investigation, October 15, 2025. Net new hiring fell from 177,000 (2021–22) to under 17,000 (2023–25). Published in Reuters, Gulf News, Business World, Business Standard and 15+ global outlets.
2. Jefferies investment bank projection: September 2025. 50% revenue impact on call centres; 35% on back-office BPO from AI within five years. India holds 52% of global outsourcing market. Source: Reuters; The420.in.
3. Vinod Khosla at India AI Impact Summit 2026, New Delhi, February 16–17, 2026: 'By 2030, there will be no such thing as IT services. There will be no such thing as BPO. Those are gone.' Sources: YourStory, BusinessToday, Business Standard (February 16–17, 2026).
4. Sam Altman at India AI Impact Summit 2026, New Delhi, February 19, 2026: Direct quotes on superintelligence timeline and intellectual capacity. Sources: Outlook India, The Tribune (ANI), Kashmir Reader, TechStory, Digit.in (February 19–21, 2026).
5. India BPO workforce 1.6 million; Tier-2 salaries ₹15,000–₹20,000/month; 70%+ BPOs using NLP/AI; RPA handles 40–50% of repetitive tasks: Astute Analytica / GlobeNewswire, April 2025.
6. The Media Ant replaced 15 salespeople and a 6-person call centre with AI agent 'Neha'. LimeChat: ₹1 lakh/month

replaces 15 agents. Haptik revenue ₹8.7 crore (2020) to ₹158 crore (2024): The420.in, October 2025.
7. NASSCOM data: 30%+ of new BPO hires in 2024 from Tier-2/3 cities; Jaipur 25,000 seats, Coimbatore 30,000, Chandigarh 20,000: Employment Mantras, May 2025.
8. India gig workforce projection 23.5 million by 2029–30: NITI Aayog; ORF Online, November 2025.
9. Solapur IT Park: 50 acres on Hotgi Road, MIDC; ₹38 crore investment; 45,000 job target: Pune Pulse, November 22, 2025; Free Press Journal, October 16, 2025. CM Devendra Fadnavis announcement. Solapur Airport inaugurated September 29, 2024.
10. 68% of Indian white-collar workers fear AI automation within five years: IIM-Ahmedabad / PMC research, 2025.

CHAPTER SEVEN: THE SAME TOOL. A DIFFERENT PAIR OF HANDS. (HEALTHCARE & ACCESS GAP)

1. Qure.ai / qXR AI chest X-ray system: PLOS Digital Health (2023) peer-reviewed validation; The Lancet AI — matching or outperforming radiologists. WHO TB screening policy update recommending AI reader as replacement in radiologist-absent settings. PATH TB REACH project, Nagpur: 10,481 presumptive TB patients screened. Ministry of Health: 27% decline in adverse TB outcomes in National TB Elimination Programme with AI-enabled tools.
2. India doctor-to-population ratio 1:1,272: National Health Profile 2024; WHO Global Health Observatory. Rural distribution: National Health Mission doctor posting data 2024.
3. eSanjeevani telemedicine: Ministry of Health and Family Welfare, 282 million consultations since launch. April 2023–November 2025: 12 million patients received AI-recommended differential diagnoses.
4. Niramai: thermal imaging breast cancer detection at rural health camps: Company publications; health technology sector reports 2024.
5. MadhuNetrAI diabetic retinopathy screening: National Programme for Control of Blindness, Ministry of Health. Ophthalmologist ratio: 1.3 per 100,000 population.

6. ASER 2024 — Annual Status of Education Report, Pratham: 649,491 children, 17,997 villages surveyed. Published January 2025.
7. Mindspark / Educational Initiatives, Ahmedabad: MIT J-PAL randomised controlled trial — 2–3x learning gains; 5–15% projected lifetime earnings increase; 400,000 children reached; $2 per child per year at scale.
8. SUVAS — Supreme Court Vidhik Anuvaad Software: 36,000+ Supreme Court judgments in Hindi; 17,000+ in 16 regional languages. Lok Sabha statement, Law Ministry, August 2024.
9. Tele-Law programme: Department of Justice, Ministry of Law and Justice. January 2025: 2.5 lakh gram panchayats, 785 districts, 1 crore+ beneficiaries.
10. AI credit scoring: MIS Quarterly (2024) study of 1 million underserved borrowers. IMF data: UPI/Aadhaar reducing bank customer acquisition cost from $12 to $0.06.
11. RAHAT disaster management AI, Cachar district, Assam: District administration documentation; 2022 flood data — 85% population affected. Google Flood Hub operational deployment across India.

CHAPTER EIGHT: THE ONES WE LEFT BEHIND (RETAIL, HEALTHCARE SUPPORT, EDUCATION, DOMESTIC WORKERS)

1. Retail sector employs 40–50 million: DPIIT / IBEF Retail Industry Report 2024.
2. Blinkit: 122% year-on-year growth in FY2024; 149 new dark stores: Zomato Q4 FY2024 Earnings Report; Mint, Economic Times, Business Standard (April–May 2024).
3. Medical transcription 99% global automation rate: MRFR Medical Transcription Market Report 2024; AHIMA workforce transition data.
4. Indian laboratory automation market: valued at more than ₹2,500 crore and growing: MRFR India Laboratory Automation Market Report 2024.
5. Private tuition 7.1 crore students enrolled: NSSO 71st Round (2016); cited in ASER and NITI Aayog education reports.
6. Coaching industry worth more than ₹58,000 crore annually: KPMG–Google India Future of Education 2021; EY India EdTech Report 2023–24.

7. ChatGPT Plus / OpenAI Study Mode: ₹1,700/month approximately; Study Mode released 2025: OpenAI pricing page; India Today Tech, The Hindu Tech (2025).
8. Domestic workers 4–5 crore: ILO India Domestic Workers Report 2021; National Sample Survey Office; NCEUS reports.
9. AI in healthcare support roles: McKinsey Global Institute 'The Future of Work in India' 2024; World Economic Forum Future of Jobs Report 2025.

CHAPTER NINE: THE PEOPLE WHO THOUGHT THEY WERE WATCHING FROM THE SHORE (WHITE COLLAR)

1. 92% AI usage among Indian knowledge workers: Microsoft–LinkedIn Work Trend Index 2024. India ranked first globally. Top uses: email drafting, meeting summaries, content rephrasing.
2. IIM Ahmedabad executive survey 2024: 60% of Indian white-collar workers believe AI will replace jobs in their sector within five years. Only 4% of Indian companies have trained more than 50% of staff in AI skills.
3. TCS 12,261 job reductions, July 2025. Revenue +1.3%, profit +5.9% same period: TCS Q1 FY2026 earnings; Business Standard, Economic Times (July 2025).
4. India IT sector: 64,000 jobs shed in FY2024; 25,000–30,000 in 2025; campus hiring fell 60%+: NASSCOM HR Summit data; Mint, Business Standard (2024–25).
5. Wipro: 200+ AI-powered intelligent agents in HR, finance, legal. Chairman Rishad Premji statement on autonomous systems: Wipro Annual Report 2024–25.
6. PhonePe: 60% reduction in customer support headcount over five years: TechPolicy Press investigation 2025; company statements.
7. Mustafa Suleyman, CEO Microsoft AI: Financial Times interview, February 13, 2026. 'White-collar work... most of those tasks will be fully automated by an AI within the next 12 to 18 months.'
8. Dario Amodei, CEO Anthropic: AI could eliminate half of entry-level white-collar jobs: Anthropic public statements; The Verge, Fortune (2025).

9. Marketing: 77% of professionals use ChatGPT. AI-generated landing pages convert 36% better; ads click-through 38% better: HubSpot State of Marketing 2024; Persado AI copy performance data.
10. Accounting: 85% of routine bookkeeping automatable: US Bureau of Labor Statistics Occupational Outlook; McKinsey 'A Future that Works' (updated 2024).
11. Legal automation: due diligence from ₹40 lakh to ₹4 lakh; contract analysis from 2 hours to 2 minutes: ROSS Intelligence, Harvey AI, Thomson Reuters Legal Tracker data.
12. HR automation: 85% of recruitment screening projected to be automated 2025–27: WEF Future of Jobs Report 2025; SHRM Automation in HR Survey 2024.
13. Vineet Nayyar, former HCL Technologies CEO quote: Business Today / Economic Times interview 2024–25.
14. Economic Survey of India 2024–25: dedicated chapter 'Labour in the AI Era: Crisis or Catalyst.'
15. ILO India Employment Report 2024: educated youth unemployment doubled from 35% in 2000 to 66% in 2022.

CHAPTER TEN: THE TERRIFIED BUSINESSMAN

1. Sam Altman quote on one-person billion-dollar company: Fortune interview / conversation with Alexis Ohanian, February 2024. Source: Fortune, February 2024.
2. Vinod Khosla at India AI Impact Summit 2026, Bharat Mandapam, New Delhi, February 17, 2026: 'By 2030, there will be no such thing as IT services...' Sources: YourStory, BusinessToday, TechCrunch (February 17, 2026).
3. WTO–ICC survey 2025: 41% of small businesses have adopted AI vs. 60%+ of large firms: WTO–International Chamber of Commerce Digital Economy Survey 2025.
4. Seven business verticals and AI automation: McKinsey Global Institute, Gartner, IDC India enterprise AI reports 2024–25.

CHAPTER ELEVEN: A WALK THROUGH TOMORROW

1. AI air conditioning optimisation, Bengaluru pilot: 17% wait time reduction 2023 verified by author research; BESCOM

(Bangalore Electricity Supply Company) smart grid pilot data.
2. V2X (Vehicle-to-Everything) infrastructure: China 700,000+ km smart road deployment; US NHTSA V2X mandate timeline: ITU-T V2X standards documentation; China Ministry of Transport report 2024.
3. Traffic congestion reduction 20%: Author's analysis based on Singapore LTA data and Mumbai MMRDA smart traffic pilot reports.
4. Smart geyser and home automation India market: CEAMA (Consumer Electronics and Appliances Manufacturers Association) India Smart Home Report 2024.
5. AI-enabled agriculture India (crop monitoring, irrigation): ICAR AI for Agriculture initiative; Ninjacart, DeHaat, Jivabhumi platform documented outcomes 2023–24.

CHAPTER TWELVE: WAKE UP

1. Displacement table aggregate numbers: Compiled from chapter-specific sources listed above. Methodology: NSSO employment data cross-referenced with sector automation timelines from industry sources, academic studies, and technology deployment reports.
2. Sam Altman keynote, India AI Impact Summit, New Delhi, February 19, 2026: 'If we are right, by the end of 2028, more of the world's intellectual capacity could reside inside of data centers than outside of them.' Sources: Outlook India, The Tribune (ANI), Kashmir Reader, TechStory, Digit.in.
3. Mustafa Suleyman, CEO Microsoft AI: Financial Times, February 13, 2026.
4. Vinod Khosla: India AI Impact Summit, Bharat Mandapam, New Delhi, February 16–17, 2026: YourStory, BusinessToday, Business Standard.
5. Skill India Mission: more than 14 million trained since 2015: Ministry of Skill Development and Entrepreneurship Annual Report 2024–25.
6. PM MITRA textile parks, PLI schemes: Ministry of Textiles; DPIIT PLI Annual Update 2024–25.
7. Rajasthan Gig Workers Act and state protections: State legislature documentation; Fairwork India 2024.

8. Digital India infrastructure (UPI, Aadhaar, JAM trinity): NPCI UPI transaction data; UIDAI Aadhaar issuance statistics; Ministry of Finance JAM Programme review 2024.
9. India spacecraft south pole of moon: ISRO Chandrayaan-3 mission documentation, August 2023.
10. India democratic elections: Election Commission of India data, General Elections 2024.

www.ingramcontent.com/pod-product-compliance
Ingram Content Group UK Ltd.
Pitfield, Milton Keynes, MK11 3LW, UK
UKHW041352190726
13845UKWH00026B/549

9 789357 597838